SPECTRUM®

Geometry

Grades 6–8

Spectrum®
an imprint of Carson-Dellosa Publishing LLC
Greensboro, NC

Spectrum® is an imprint of Carson-Dellosa Publishing.

Printed in the United States of America. All rights reserved. Except as permitted under the United States Copyright Act, no part of this publication may be reproduced or distributed in any form or by any means, or stored in a database or retrieval system, without prior written permission from the publisher, unless otherwise indicated. Spectrum® is an imprint of Carson-Dellosa Publishing. © 2011 Carson-Dellosa Publishing.

Send all inquiries to:
Carson-Dellosa Publishing
P.O. Box 35665
Greensboro, NC 27425 USA

Printed in the USA   ISBN 978-0-7696-6326-5

05-238137811

Table of Contents Geometry

Table of Contents, continued

Chapter 9 Volume

Check What You Know

Points, Lines, Rays, and Angles

1. Under each of the following items, write line, line segment, or ray. Then, circle the correct names. Each has more than one correct name.

a	**b**	**c**

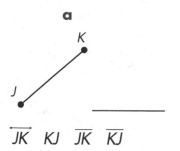 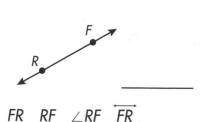 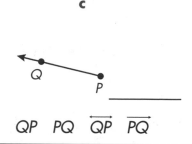

$\overrightarrow{JK}$ KJ $\overline{JK}$ $\overline{KJ}$ FR RF $\angle RF$ $\overrightarrow{FR}$ QP PQ $\overleftrightarrow{QP}$ $\overrightarrow{PQ}$

2. In the list below, circle the collinear points in the lines on the right.

ABG ABC FBG ABE

DBE CBG GBF CBF

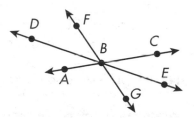

3. Name the angles that have *L* as their vertex.

_____ _____ _____

4. Name ∠5 in two different ways.

_____ _____

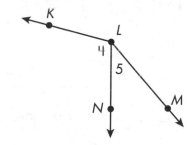

5. Use a protractor to find the measure of each angle. Circle the type of angle below.

a	**b**	**c**

angle: _____   angle: _____   angle: _____

right, acute, obtuse   right, acute, obtuse   right, acute, obtuse

Check What You Know

Points, Lines, Rays, and Angles

Use the figure to complete the following.

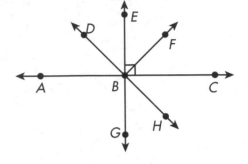

6. Name an angle that is vertical to ∠ABD.

_____

7. Name an angle that is vertical to ∠GBH.

_____

8. Name an angle that is supplementary to ∠EBC. _____

9. ∠EBC is 90°. $\overrightarrow{BF}$ bisects ∠EBC. What is the angle measure of ∠EBF? _____

10. Name an angle that is complementary to ∠FBC. _____

Use the figure to complete the following.

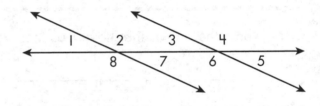

11. Name the alternate interior angles.

∠_____ / ∠_____

∠_____ / ∠_____

12. Name the alternate exterior angles.

∠_____ / ∠_____   ∠_____ / ∠_____

13. ∠1 and ∠2 are adjacent. If ∠2 is 155°, what is the measure of ∠1? _____

Use the figure to complete the following.

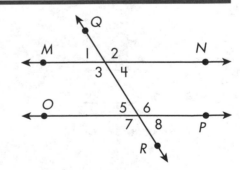

14. Name the transversal of $\overleftrightarrow{MN}$ and $\overleftrightarrow{OP}$. _____

15. ∠1 and ∠8 are congruent. If ∠1 is 60°, what is the measure of ∠8? _____

16. Name a corresponding angle to ∠8. _____

Lesson 1.1 Points and Lines

A **point** has no dimensions but defines a location in space.

Point *R* is shown at right.

A **line** extends infinitely in both directions.

Line *ST* is the same as line *TS* and can also be named $\overleftrightarrow{ST}$ or $\overleftrightarrow{TS}$.

A **line segment** is the part of the line between two **end points**.

Segment *UV* is the same as segment *VU* and can also be named $\overline{UV}$ or $\overline{VU}$.

Name the following figures. Number 1 is given.

		a	**b**
1.	A ———— B	line *AB* or *BA*	$\overleftrightarrow{AB}$ or $\overleftrightarrow{BA}$
2.	C —— D	line ____ or ____	_____ or _____
3.	E —— F	line ____ or ____	_____ or _____

		a	**b**	**c**
4.	G —— H	line segment *GH* or ___	$\overline{GH}$ or ____	endpoints ____ and ____
5.	J —— K	line segment *JK* or ____	$\overline{JK}$ or ____	endpoints ____ and ____

Draw the following figures.

	a	**b**
6.	line *LM*	$\overrightarrow{PQ}$
7.	$\overline{RS}$	$\overline{TU}$

Lesson 1.1 Points and Lines

Collinear points are three or more points on the same straight line.

Points that do not appear on the same straight line are **noncollinear**.

A **midpoint** is the point halfway between the end points on a line segment. On the line *WY* at right, the midpoint is *X*.

1. In the list below, circle the collinear points in the lines on the right. (There is more than one correct answer.)

    MKL

    MKJ

    MKN

    JKL

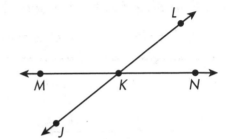

2. In the list below, circle the collinear points in the lines on the right. (There is more than one correct answer.)

    ABC

    BDG

    ABD

    DBC

    EDG

    ADE

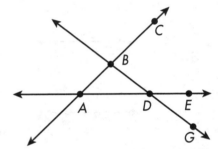

3. In the list below, circle the correct names for the item on the right.

    $\overleftrightarrow{LM}$ ML $\overleftarrow{ML}$ LM

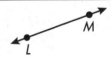

4. Draw a line segment using the points on the right, and then name it in the space below.

    N

    O

    _____

Lesson 1.2 Rays and Angles

A **ray** is a part of a line. It has <u>one</u> endpoint but extends infinitely in one direction. At right is ray WX or $\overrightarrow{WX}$. It is *not* ray XW.

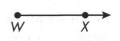

See angle YWX at right. An **angle** is the union of two rays that share a common endpoint. The two rays that make up the angle are called the **sides**. The endpoint (W) is called a **vertex**.

At right is angle YWX. It is the union of $\overrightarrow{WX}$ and $\overrightarrow{WY}$. Angle YWX can be written as $\angle XWY$, $\angle YWX$, or $\angle W$. The vertex ($\angle W$) stands for the angle.

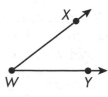

At right is an angle formed by the union of $\overrightarrow{CA}$ and $\overrightarrow{CE}$. Write it

$\angle ACE$, $\angle ECA$, or $\angle C$. It could also be called angle 4.

Complete the following. The first answer is given.

	a	**b**

1. ray CD $\overrightarrow{CD}$ endpoint C

2. ray _____ _____   endpoint _____

3. ray _____ _____   endpoint _____

Name each figure using letters. Name each figure in more than one way, if you can.

4. _____

5. _____

Lesson 1.2 Rays and Angles

In the figure at right, you can see there are three angles with the same vertex. The common vertex is A.

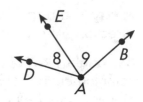

When you have more than one angle at a vertex, use three points to name an angle. The vertex is always the middle letter. You can also refer to the angle with a number.

For example, you can name the angle ∠8 as ∠DAE or ∠EAD. You can name angle ∠9 as ∠EAB or ∠BAE. The third angle in the figure to the right is ∠DAB, or ∠BAD.

Complete the following. The first answer is given.

1. angles: ∠NLM   ∠MLN   ∠L ∠4

    vertex: L   sides: $\overrightarrow{LM}$ $\overrightarrow{LN}$

    rays: $\overrightarrow{LM}$ $\overrightarrow{LN}$

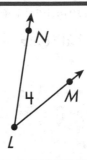

---

2. angles: _____ _____ _____ _____

    vertex: _____   sides: _____ _____

    rays: _____ _____

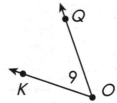

---

3. Name the angles that have A as their vertex.

    _____ _____ _____

4. Name the sides of ∠EAC.

    _____ _____

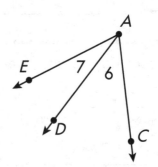

Lesson 1.3 Measuring Angles

Use a protractor to measure angles. Place the center point of the protractor on the vertex of the angle you want to measure.

The measure of a **right angle** is 90°.

The measure of an **acute angle** is less than 90°.

The measure of an **obtuse angle** is greater than 90°.

The measure of ∠XYZ is 50°.

right angle	obtuse angle	acute angle

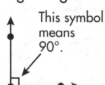

This symbol means 90°.

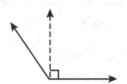

Find the measure of each angle. Write whether the angle is right, acute, or obtuse.

a   **b**

1.

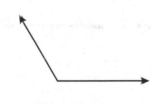

_____ _____   _____ _____

2.

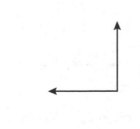

_____ _____   _____ _____

Lesson 1.4 Vertical, Supplementary, and Complementary Angles

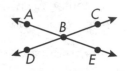

Vertical angles are opposite angles that have the same measure. ∠ABC and ∠DBE are vertical. Vertical angles are **congruent** since they have the same measure.

Supplementary angles are two angles whose measures have a sum of 180°. ∠ABD and ∠DBE are supplementary.

Complementary angles are two angles whose measures have a sum of 90°. ∠WXZ and ∠ZXY are complementary.

A **bisector** divides an angle into two angles of equal measure. XZ is the bisector of ∠WXY.

Use the figure to the right to answer questions 1–4.

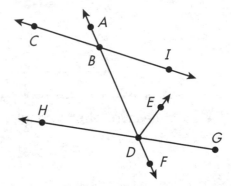

1. Name an angle that is vertical to ∠ABC. _____

2. Name an angle that is vertical to ∠HDB. _____

3. Name an angle that is supplementary to ∠GDF. _____

4. Name the bisector of ∠ADG. _____

Use the figure to the right to answer questions 5 and 6.

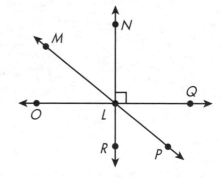

5. Name an angle that is complementary to ∠MLN.

   _____

6. Name an angle that is complementary to ∠PLR.

   _____

Solve.

7. ∠ABC is supplementary to ∠CBD. The measure of ∠ABC is 63°. What is the measure of ∠CBD? _____

8. ∠MNO is complementary to ∠OND. The measure of ∠MNO is 82°. What is the measure of ∠OND? _____

Lesson 1.5 Transversals

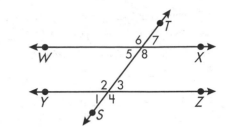

Parallel lines are two lines that will never meet. In the figure, $\overleftrightarrow{WX}$ and $\overleftrightarrow{YZ}$ are parallel lines.

A **transversal** is a line that intersects two parallel lines. $\overleftrightarrow{ST}$ is a transversal of $\overleftrightarrow{YZ}$ and $\overleftrightarrow{WX}$.

Corresponding angles are formed when a transversal intersects parallel lines. Corresponding angles are angles ∠1 and ∠5, ∠2 and ∠6, ∠3 and ∠7, and ∠4 and ∠8.

Adjacent angles are any two angles that are next to one another, such as ∠1/∠2 and ∠2/∠3. Adjacent angles share a ray. They form supplementary angles (180°).

---

1. Name the pairs of adjacent angles in the figure.

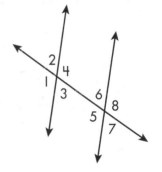

∠___/∠___, ∠___/∠___, ∠___/∠___, ∠___/∠___,

∠___/∠___, ∠___/∠___, ∠___/∠___, ∠___/∠___,

Alternate interior angles are those that are inside the parallel lines and opposite one another. ∠3 and ∠6 are alternate interior angles. They are congruent.

2. Name another pair of alternate interior angles in the figure.
∠_____/∠_____

Alternate exterior angles are those that are outside the parallel lines and opposite one another. ∠1 and ∠8 are alternate exterior angles. They are congruent.

3. Name another pair of alternate exterior angles in the figure. ∠_____/∠_____

List the following pairs of angles in the figure.

4. Adjacent:

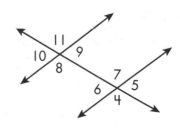

∠___/∠___, ∠___/∠___, ∠___/∠___, ∠___/∠___,

∠___/∠___, ∠___/∠___, ∠___/∠___, ∠___/∠___,

5. Alternate interior: ∠_____/∠_____, ∠_____/∠_____

6. Alternate exterior: ∠_____/∠_____, ∠_____/∠_____

Lesson 1.6 Drawing Angles

You can draw angles using a protractor. See the figure to the right. The center point of the protractor will be the vertex of the angle you want to draw.

Y is the vertex. $\overrightarrow{YZ}$ is at 0°. Draw a line from the vertex to the degree mark on the protractor. $\angle XYZ$ is 90°.

To draw $\overrightarrow{YW}$, find the degree mark and draw the line from the vertex.

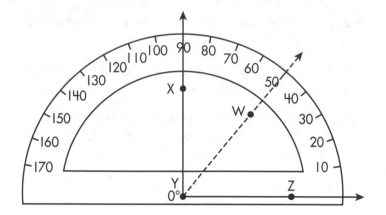

Draw the angle in the space to the right of each problem. Answer the questions.

1. Draw $\angle ABC$ at 70°. Draw an angle bisector $\overrightarrow{BD}$.

    What is the measure of $\angle ABD$? _____

    What is the measure of $\angle DBC$? _____

2. Draw $\angle EFG$ at 120°. Draw $\overrightarrow{FH}$ at 50°.

    What is the measure of $\angle EFH$? _____

    Is $\angle EFG$ right, acute, or obtuse? _____

3. Draw $\angle JKL$ at 90°. Draw $\overrightarrow{KM}$ at 30°.

    What is the measure of $\angle JKM$? _____

    Is $\angle JKM$ vertical, supplementary, or complementary? _____

Check What You Learned

Points, Lines, Rays, and Angles

1. Under each of the following items, write *line*, *line segment*, or *ray*. Then, circle the correct names. Each has more than one correct name.

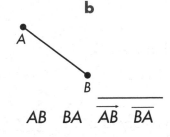

a

$\overrightarrow{ED}$ $\overrightarrow{DE}$ $\overline{DE}$ DE

b

AB BA $\overrightarrow{AB}$ $\overline{BA}$

c

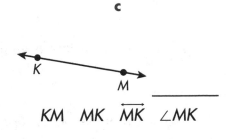

KM MK $\overleftrightarrow{MK}$ ∠MK

2. In the list below, circle the collinear points in the lines on the right.

ABF   CBA
DBE   CBG
FBE   ABC
GBD   FBC

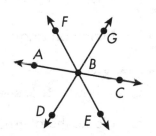

3. Name the angles that have *P* as their vertex.

_____ _____ _____

4. Name ∠8 in two different ways.

_____ _____

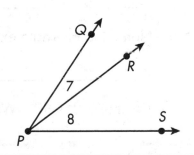

5. Use a protractor to find the measure of each angle. Circle right, acute, or obtuse.

a

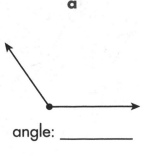

angle: _____

right, acute, obtuse

b

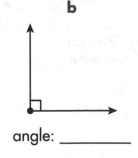

angle: _____

right, acute, obtuse

c

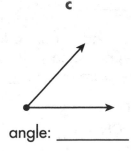

angle: _____

right, acute, obtuse

Check What You Learned

Points, Lines, Rays, and Angles

Use the figure to answer the following.

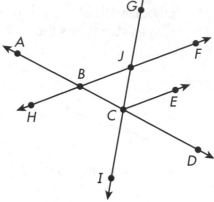

6. Name an angle that is vertical to ∠BJC.

_____

7. Name an angle that is vertical to ∠ACG.

_____

8. Name an angle that is supplementary to ∠JCD. _____

9. ∠DCJ is 90°. $\overrightarrow{CE}$ bisects ∠DCJ. What is the angle measure of ∠DCE? _____

10. Name an angle that is complementary to ∠DCE. _____

Use the figure to answer the following.

11. Name the alternate interior angles.

∠_____/∠_____   ∠_____/∠_____

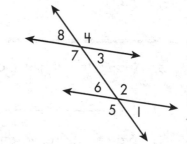

12. Name the alternate exterior angles.

∠_____/∠_____   ∠_____/∠_____

13. Assume ∠8 is 40°. What is the measure of ∠1? _____

Use the figure to answer the following.

14. Name the transversal of $\overleftrightarrow{AC}$ and $\overleftrightarrow{DF}$.

_____

15. ∠1 and ∠4 are adjacent angles. They are supplementary. If ∠4 is 150°, what is the measure of ∠1? _____

16. If ∠4 is 150°, what is the measure of ∠DEH? _____

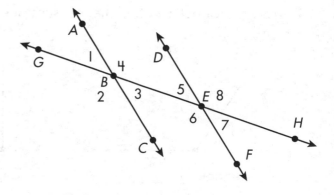

Check What You Know

Ratios and Proportion

Cross-multiply to see if the ratios form a true proportion, or equality of ratios. Write *T* next to proportions that are true.

	a	**b**	**c**
1.	$\frac{1}{4} = \frac{3}{12}$ _____	$\frac{3}{5} = \frac{7}{10}$ _____	$\frac{5}{8} = \frac{8}{5}$ _____
2.	1 to 3 = 7 to 21 _____	4 to 3 = 16 to 12 _____	2:6 = 6:18 _____
3.	5:7 = 15:21 _____	5 to 1 = 20 to 5 _____	$\frac{3}{13} = \frac{9}{39}$ _____
4.	0:5 = $\frac{4}{3}$ _____	3 to 11 = 3:33 _____	$\frac{2}{7}$ = 6 to 21 _____

Solve for *n* in each proportion.

5.	$\frac{2}{5} = \frac{n}{15}$ _____	4:3 = 16:n _____	8 to 1 = n to 8 _____
6.	$\frac{n}{11} = \frac{4}{2}$ _____	6 to n = 54 to 9 _____	$\frac{1}{8} = \frac{n}{24}$ _____
7.	3:5 = 6:n _____	n to 12 = 4 to 3 _____	19 to n = $\frac{5}{2}$ _____
8.	n:12 = 2 to 3 _____	$\frac{26}{n}$ = 39:3 _____	50:5 = 22 to n _____

NAME _____

Check What You Know

Ratios and Proportion

Write a proportion for each problem. Then, solve the problem.

9. Torrez Motors sells 1 truck for every 5 cars it sells. This month, Torrez predicts that it will sell 25 cars. How many trucks does the company expect to sell this month?

_____ Torrez Motors expects to sell _____ trucks.

10. The ratio of girls to boys in the school band is 2 to 3. There are 6 girls in the band. How many boys are in the band?

_____ There are _____ boys in the band.

11. Sam's Shoes makes a profit of $38 on every pair of athletic shoes it sells. How many pairs of shoes must Sam's sell to earn a profit of $950?

_____ Sam's must sell _____ pairs of shoes.

12. A map of a bike trail uses a scale of 2 inches for every 3 miles. The scale drawing of the trail was 15 inches long. How long is the bike trail?

_____ The bike trail is _____ miles long.

13. A painting shows a tree that is 6 inches tall. The tree is actually 18 feet tall. In the artist's scale, how many feet did each inch of the painting represent?

_____ The scale is _____ feet per inch.

14. A rectangle has a length of 16 inches and a width of 7 inches. What number represents the rectangle's proportion of length to width? Round to hundredths.

_____ The proportion of length to width is _____.

Lesson 2.1 Ratio and Proportion

A **ratio** is a comparison of 2 numbers. A ratio can be expressed as 1 to 2, 1:2, or $\frac{1}{2}$. In this example, the ratio means that for every 1 of the first item, there are 2 of the other item.

A **proportion** expresses the equality of 2 ratios. Cross-multiply to determine if two ratios are equal.

$\frac{4}{2} \bowtie \frac{2}{1}$ $4 \times 1 = 2 \times 2$, so the proportion is true.

$\frac{3}{4} = \frac{2}{3}$ $3 \times 3 \neq 4 \times 2$, so the proportion is **not** true.

Cross-multiply to check each proportion. Show your work. Write *T* next to proportions that are true.

	a	**b**	**c**
1.	$\frac{1}{2} = \frac{3}{6}$ _____	$\frac{5}{8} = \frac{3}{10}$ _____	$\frac{1}{3} = \frac{3}{9}$ _____
2.	$4:9 = 9:4$ _____	$\frac{3}{18} = \frac{1}{6}$ _____	$2 \text{ to } 5 = 5 \text{ to } 12$ _____
3.	$\frac{1}{4} = \frac{11}{44}$ _____	$6 \text{ to } 3 = 7 \text{ to } 6$ _____	$\frac{6}{7} = \frac{18}{21}$ _____
4.	$\frac{3}{2} = 6:3$ _____	$4 \text{ to } 3 = 20:15$ _____	$\frac{4}{3} = \frac{16}{9}$ _____
5.	$10:12 = \frac{30}{36}$ _____	$\frac{3}{8} = \frac{9}{24}$ _____	$\frac{13}{26} = \frac{1}{2}$ _____
6.	$\frac{3}{4} = \frac{9}{14}$ _____	$5:3 = \frac{11}{7}$ _____	$\frac{3}{6} = \frac{8}{4}$ _____
7.	$\frac{7}{5} = \frac{35}{25}$ _____	$3:16 = 9:48$ _____	$\frac{9}{6} = \frac{14}{8}$ _____

Lesson 2.2 Solving Proportion Equations

You can use a proportion to solve problems.

The ratio of apples to oranges in a basket is 4 to 5. There are 20 oranges in the basket. How many apples are there?

$\frac{4}{5} = \frac{n}{20}$ Set up a proportion, using n for the missing number.

$4 \times 20 = 5 \times n$ Cross-multiply.

$\frac{80}{5} = n$ Solve for n.

$16 = n$ There are 16 apples.

The missing number can appear anyplace in a proportion. Solve the same way.

$\frac{2}{3} = \frac{6}{n}$ $\frac{n}{4} = \frac{3}{6}$

$3 \times 6 = 2 \times n$ $4 \times 3 = 6 \times n$

$\frac{18}{2} = n$ $\frac{12}{6} = n$

$9 = n$ $2 = n$

Solve for n in each proportion.

               a   **b**   **c**

1. $\frac{3}{4} = \frac{n}{16}$ _____ $3:5 = n:20$ _____ $\frac{1}{7} = \frac{9}{n}$ _____

2. $\frac{n}{8} = \frac{5}{2}$ _____ $18:n = 6:3$ _____ 2 to $6 = 20$ to n _____

3. $\frac{n}{11} = \frac{5}{55}$ _____ $\frac{4}{n} = \frac{16}{10}$ _____ $n:18 = 3:27$ _____

Write a proportion for each problem. Then, solve the problem.

4. Emilio wants to make a pumpkin pie for each of his 5 cousins. One pie requires 15 ounces of pumpkin filling. How many ounces of filling must Emilio buy?

_____ Emilio must buy _____ ounces of filling.

5. Julia owns a home worth $100,000. She must pay $5 in property tax for every $1,000 of her home's value. How much property tax will Julia pay?

_____ Julia will pay _____ in property tax.

Lesson 2.3 Proportions and Scale Drawings

A **scale drawing** is a drawing of a real object in which all of the dimensions are proportional to the real object. A scale drawing can be larger or smaller than the object it represents. The **scale** is the ratio of the drawing size to the actual size of the object.

A drawing of a person has a scale of 2 inches = 1 foot. If the drawing is 11 inches high, how tall is the person?

$$\frac{2}{1} = \frac{11}{n}$$ Write a proportion.

$1 \times 11 = n \times 2$ Solve for n.

$5\frac{1}{2} = n$ The person is $5\frac{1}{2}$ feet tall.

Write a proportion for each problem. Then, solve the problem.

1. A map of Ohio uses a scale of 1 inch = 11 miles. The map is 20 inches wide. How wide is Ohio?

    _____ Ohio is _____ miles wide.

2. The Statue of Liberty is 305 feet tall. A scale drawing has a ratio of 1 inch = 5 feet. How tall is the drawing?

    _____ The drawing is _____ inches tall.

3. A customer asked Lan's Photo Shop to enlarge a photograph to make a poster 24 inches long. The original photo is 6 inches long. How many inches will the shop enlarge the photo for every inch of the original length?

    _____ The enlargement will be _____ inches for every inch.

4. A landscape designer made a scale drawing of a client's yard. The scale is 2 inches to 5 feet. The yard is 70 feet wide. How wide is the drawing?

    _____ The drawing is _____ inches wide.

5. A coach uses a scale drawing of a soccer field to design plays. The drawing is 27.5 centimeters long. The scale is 1 centimeter to 4 meters. How long is the soccer field?

    _____ The soccer field is _____ meters long.

Lesson 2.4 The Golden Ratio

A special ratio of length to width appears in many works of art and architecture. This **golden ratio** is approximately 1.618. The Greek letter *phi*, φ, represents the golden ratio. Many artists and architects since the early Greeks believed that the golden ratio makes the most beautiful shapes.

A rectangle with a ratio of length to width of 1.618 is called a **golden rectangle**. A property of a golden rectangle is that the ratio of (length + width) to length equals the ratio of length to width.

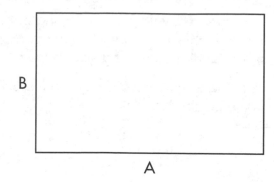

$$\frac{A}{B} = \frac{A+B}{A} = 1.618 = \varphi$$

Find the rectangular items listed in the table below in your home, school, or library. Measure them. Write the length and width of each item in the table. Then, complete the table by determining the ratio.

Item	Length (inches)	Width (inches)	Ratio (L/W)
Picture Frame			
Computer Screen			
Textbook			
Sheet of Paper			

1. Which item in the table has a ratio closest to the golden ratio? _____

2. If a golden rectangle has a length of 6 feet, what is its width? Write a proportion for this problem. Then, solve for the missing width. Round to hundredths.

   _____ The width is _____ feet.

3. Use the length and width from question 2 to determine if $\frac{A+B}{A}$ also equals the golden ratio. Round to hundredths.

   A _____ + B _____ = _____ ÷ A _____ = _____

Check What You Learned

Ratios and Proportion

Cross-multiply to check each proportion. Show your work. Write *T* next to proportions that are true.

	a	**b**	**c**

1. $\frac{5}{7} = \frac{3}{5}$ _____ $\frac{2}{3} = \frac{100}{150}$ _____ $\frac{9}{8} = \frac{11}{9}$ _____

2.   13:16 = 4:5 _____   7:8 = 14:16 _____   1 to 5 = 17 to 85 _____

3. $\frac{3}{8} = \frac{12}{32}$ _____   3 to 2 = 29 to 18 _____ $\frac{7}{9}$ = 18 to 23 _____

4.   10:3 = $\frac{30}{9}$ _____   82:6 = $\frac{41}{3}$ _____   11 to 12 = 6 to 8 _____

Solve for *n* in each proportion.

5. $\frac{16}{3} = \frac{n}{6}$ _____   3:4 = 6:n _____   n to 5 = 30 to 50 _____

6.   12:n = 36:12 _____ $\frac{3}{10}$ = n to 14 _____   n:21 = 8 to 3 _____

7. $\frac{2}{15} = \frac{6}{n}$ _____   5:n = 3:18 _____   n to 50 = 2 to 2.5 _____

8.   104:4 = 26:n _____ $\frac{n}{45}$ = 5:15 _____   2:n = $\frac{19}{28.5}$ _____

Check What You Learned

Ratios and Proportion

Write a proportion for each problem. Then, solve the problem.

9. Carmen ran 5 kilometers in 32 minutes. How many minutes did it take her to run 1 kilometer?

_____ Carmen ran 1 kilometer in _____ minutes.

10. Matt wants to make his trail mix in a proportion of 1 pound of raisins for every 4 pounds of nuts. He put 0.8 pounds of nuts into a bag. How many pounds of raisins should he add?

_____ Matt should add _____ pounds of raisins.

11. Kwan's car uses 15 gallons of gas to go 390 miles. How many miles does Kwan's car travel per gallon of gas?

_____ Kwan's car travels _____ miles per gallon of gas.

12. A park is 15 miles wide. On a scale drawing, the park is 10 inches wide. How many miles does 2 inches represent on the map?

_____ Two inches represent _____ miles on the map.

13. A photograph shows a lizard 5 inches long. The photo uses a scale of 0.5:2. How long is the actual lizard?

_____ The lizard is _____ inches long.

14. An artist created a painting in the shape of a golden rectangle. If the length of the painting is 60 centimeters, what is the width? Round to hundredths.

_____ The width is _____ centimeters.

Check What You Know

Finding Angles with Algebra

Identify the coefficient and the variable in each term below.

a	**b**

1. 23n coefficient _____ variable _____   y coefficient _____ variable _____

Write each item as an expression, equation, or inequality. Use *n* for an unknown number.

2. three 5s are greater than a number   a number divided by 3, increased by 2

_____   _____

Underline the operation that should be done first. Then, find the value of the equation.

3.   4 × 3 ÷ 6 = _____   12 × (5 − 2) = _____

4.   9 + 6 ÷ 3 = _____   [14 ÷ (2 + 5)] + 8 = _____

Name the property that each equation illustrates. The properties are commutative, associative, identity, or zero.

5. 7 × 3 = 3 × 7 _____   0 ÷ g = 0 _____

6.   k + 0 = k _____   6 + (9 + 5) = (6 + 9) + 5 _____

Rewrite each expression using the distributive property.

7.   6 × (5 + 4) _____   (p × 3) − (p × 2) _____

8.   7d + 7e _____   (r − 8) × 5 _____

NAME _____

 Check What You Know

Finding Angles with Algebra

Find the value of each expression. Round to four decimal places, if needed.

	a	**b**	**c**
9.	2^4 _____	$3^3 \times 3^2$ _____	$6^8 \div 6^5$ _____
10.	5^{-2} _____	$2^{-2} \times 2^{-4}$ _____	$3^{-5} \div 3^{-3}$ _____

Find the measure of the complement to each angle.

11. 60° _____   25° _____   45° _____

Find the measure of the supplement to each angle.

12. 110° _____   80° _____   128° _____

Find the value of the variable in each equation.

13. $25 - n = 4$ _____ $p + 17 = 28$ _____ $8 \times z = 48$ _____

14. $h \div 6 = 12$ _____ $24 = k - 16$ _____ $18 \div r = 3$ _____

Write an equation for this problem. Then, find the value of the variable.

15. Sara took $25.36 to the store. She returned home with $5.29 in her pocket. How much money did Sara spend at the store?

_____ Sara spent _____ at the store.

Lesson 3.1 Variables, Expressions, and Equations

An **equation** is a number sentence that contains an equals sign. An **expression** is a number phrase without an equals sign. An **inequality** shows how 2 numbers or phrases compare to one another. The inequality "2 < 4" means "2 is less than 4." The inequality "5 > 3" means "5 is greater than 3."

Equations, expressions, and inequalities may contain numerals, variables, or both. A **variable** is a symbol, usually a letter, that stands for an unknown number. A **coefficient** is a number that multiplies a variable. In the variable equation below, 2 is the coefficient of the variable n. In the variable expression $a - 5$, the coefficient of a is 1.

	Equation	Expression	Inequality
Numerical	$3 \times 5 = 15$	$9 + 2$	$17 < 20$
Variable	$2n + 4 = 18$	$a - 5$	$12 > 3d$

Identify each of the following as an equation, expression, or inequality.

	a	b	c
1.	$6 - 5$ _____	$3 + 2 = 5$ _____	$8 > 4$ _____
2.	$c - 2 < 7$ _____	$y + 3$ _____	$17 = 2a + 7$ _____

For each term below, identify the coefficient and the variable.

	a		b
3.	$4b$ coefficient _____ variable _____	x	coefficient _____ variable _____
4.	$3m + 1$ coefficient _____ variable _____	$2 - 7p$	coefficient _____ variable _____

Write each item as an expression, equation, or inequality. Use n for an unknown number.

5. 7 increased by a number is 8   a number is less than 10

_____   _____

6. three 6s are greater than a number   five times a number, decreased by 7

_____   _____

Lesson 3.2 The Order of Operations

If an expression has more than one operation, you must complete the operations in a certain order. Follow this order of operations to find the value of an expression:

1. Do operations within parentheses and brackets, innermost first.

2. Multiply and divide in order from left to right.

3. Add and subtract in order from left to right.

$$4 + [12 \div (10 - 6)] \times 2 = 4 + [12 \div 4] \times 2 \qquad \text{Subtract } (10 - 6).$$
$$= 4 + 3 \times 2 \qquad \text{Divide } [12 \div 4].$$
$$= 4 + 6 \qquad \text{Multiply } 3 \times 2.$$
$$= 10 \qquad \text{Add } 4 + 6.$$

Underline the operation that should be done first. Then, find the value of the equation.

	a	**b**
1.	$11 + 4 - 3 =$ _____	$8 \times 9 \div 3 =$ _____
2.	$14 - 2 \times 3 =$ _____	$15 \div 5 - 2 =$ _____
3.	$6 \times 2 + 9 \div 3 =$ _____	$10 \times (3 + 7) =$ _____
4.	$66 \div 11 - 3 - 2 =$ _____	$66 \div (11 - 3 - 2) =$ _____
5.	$10 + 4 \times 6 \div 2 =$ _____	$(10 + 4) \times 6 \div 2 =$ _____
6.	$18 \div 2 + 7 \times 3 =$ _____	$[18 \div (2 + 7)] \times 3 =$ _____
7.	$(15 - 8) \times 2 + 12 =$ _____	$(15 - 8) \times (2 + 12) =$ _____

Lesson 3.3 Number Properties

Commutative Property: The order in which you add numbers does not change the sum. The order in which you multiply numbers does not change the product.

$$a + b = b + a$$

$$a \times b = b \times a$$

Associative Property: The way you group addends does not change the sum. The way you group factors does not change the product.

$$a + (b + c) = (a + b) + c$$

$$a \times (b \times c) = (a \times b) \times c$$

Identity Property: The sum of an addend and 0 is the addend. The product of a factor and 1 is the factor.

$$a + 0 = a \qquad a \times 1 = a$$

Properties of Zero: The product of a factor and 0 is 0. The quotient of the dividend 0 and any divisor is 0.

$$a \times 0 = 0 \qquad 0 \div a = 0$$

Name the property that each equation illustrates.

	a	**b**
1.	$9 \times n = n \times 9$ _____	$r \times 1 = r$ _____
2.	$(a + b) + c = a + (b + c)$ _____	$17 + 0 = 17$ _____
3.	$53 \times 0 = 0$ _____	$6 \times 7 \times 8 = 7 \times 8 \times 6$ _____

Rewrite each expression using the property indicated.

4.   identity: $1 \times 28 =$ _____   commutative: $n \times 5p =$ _____

5.   zero: $0 \div 21d =$ _____   associative: $(w + 9) + 7 =$ _____

6.   associative: $2f + (g + h) =$ _____   identity: $44y + 0 =$ _____

7.   zero: $(a + b + c) \times 0 =$ _____   associative: $(4fg \times 6g) \times 9 =$ _____

Lesson 3.4 The Distributive Property

The **Distributive Property** combines multiplication with addition and subtraction. This property states that:

$$a \times (b + c) = (a \times b) + (a \times c)$$
$$a \times (b - c) = (a \times b) - (a \times c)$$

$$3 \times (6 + 4) = (3 \times 6) + (3 \times 4)$$
$$3 \times (10) = (18) + (12)$$
$$30 = 30$$

Rewrite each expression using the distributive property.

	a	**b**
1.	$9 \times (3 - 1) =$ _____	$p \times (q + r) =$ _____
2.	$(6 \times 7) + (6 \times 8) =$ _____	$(15 - 3) \times 4 =$ _____
3.	$7y + 7z =$ _____	$m \times (9 - 2 - p) =$ _____
4.	$(c + d) \times h =$ _____	$(r \times r) - (r \times y) =$ _____

Write each missing number.

5. $(5 \times 3) + (n \times 2) = 5 \times (3 + 2)$ _____ $n \times (9 - 4) = (6 \times 9) - (6 \times 4)$ _____

6. $(6 - n) \times 4 = (6 \times 4) - (1 \times 4)$ _____ $(5 \times 9) + (5 \times 3) = 5 \times (9 + n)$ _____

7. $8n + 9n = 12 \times (8 + 9)$ _____ $(n \times 7) - (n \times 6) = 7 \times (7 - 6)$ _____

Lesson 3.5 Solving Addition and Subtraction Equations

Addition Property of Equality: When you add the same number to both sides of an equation, the two sides remain equal.

$$a = b \qquad a + c = b + c$$

$$4 + 2 = 6 \qquad 4 + 2 + 3 = 6 + 3 \quad [9 = 9]$$

Subtraction Property of Equality: When you subtract the same number from both sides of an equation, the two sides remain equal.

$$a = b \qquad a - c = b - c$$

$$5 = 4 + 1 \qquad 5 - 2 = 4 + 1 - 2 \quad [3 = 3]$$

Use these properties to find the value of variables.

$$a - 11 = 6 \qquad\qquad b + 3 = 14$$

$$a - 11 + 11 = 6 + 11 \qquad b + 3 - 3 = 14 - 3$$

$$a = 17 \qquad\qquad b = 11$$

Find the value of the variable in each equation.

	a	**b**	**c**
1.	$9 + n = 13$ _____	$21 - z = 10$ _____	$y + 8 = 8$ _____
2.	$29 + p = 34$ _____	$19 = b - 3$ _____	$16 + c = 43$ _____
3.	$39 = f - 62$ _____	$y + 23 = 86$ _____	$44 - g = 27$ _____

Write an equation for each problem. Then, find the value of the variable.

4. Tyra scored 38 points in three basketball games. She scored 14 points the first game and 8 points the second game. How many points did Tyra score in the third game?

_____ Tyra scored _____ points in the third game.

5. Jorge deposited $25.30 into his savings account at the bank. He now has $52.27 in his account. How much was in the account before Jorge made his deposit?

_____ Jorge had _____ in his account.

Lesson 3.6 Solving Multiplication and Division Equations

Division Property of Equality: When you divide each side of an equation by the same number, the two sides remain equal.

$$a = b$$
$$a \div c = b \div c$$
$$\frac{a}{c} = \frac{b}{c}$$

Multiplication Property of Equality: When you multiply each side of an equation by the same number, the two sides remain equal.

$$a = b$$
$$a \times c = b \times c$$

Use these properties to find the value of variables:

$$n \div 5 = 4 \qquad\qquad 3 \times n = 15 \qquad\qquad 60 \div n = 4$$

$$n \div 5 \times 5 = 4 \times 5 \qquad \frac{3 \times n}{3} = \frac{15}{3} \qquad\qquad \frac{60n}{n} = 4n \text{ or } 60 = 4n$$

$$n = 20 \qquad\qquad\qquad n = 5 \qquad\qquad\qquad \frac{60}{4} = \frac{4n}{4} \qquad 15 = n$$

Find the value of the variable in each equation.

a	b	c

1. $3 \times n = 18$ _____ $p \times 4 = 48$ _____ $b \div 6 = 5$ _____

2. $9z = 108$ _____ $13 = \frac{m}{4}$ _____ $\frac{195}{k} = 13$ _____

3. $144 \div p = 72$ _____ $m \times 34 = 476$ _____ $125 = 5h$ _____

Write an equation for each problem. Then, find the value of the variable.

4. Yu worked 20 hours this week. He worked the same number of hours each day for 5 days. How many hours did Yu work each day?

_____ Yu worked _____ hours each day.

5. A cargo van can hold 55 cartons of cereal. Franklin Cargo Company must transport 605 cartons. How many vans must the company use to do this job?

_____ The company must use _____ vans.

Lesson 3.7 Multiplying and Dividing Powers

A **power** is a number that is expressed using an **exponent**. The **base** is the number that is multiplied. The exponent tells how many times the base is used as a factor.

base   exponent

$$2^3 = 2 \times 2 \times 2 = 8$$

To multiply powers with the same base, combine bases, add the exponents, and then simplify.

$$2^2 \times 2^3 = 2^{2+3} = 2^5 = 32$$

To divide powers with the same base, combine bases, subtract exponents, and then simplify.

$$3^5 \div 3^2 = 3^{5-2} = 3^3 = 27$$

Find the value of each expression.

	a	b	c
1.	$5^3 =$ _____	$9^4 =$ _____	$2^6 =$ _____
2.	$12^2 =$ _____	$3^5 =$ _____	$17^4 =$ _____
3.	$26^3 =$ _____	$10^3 =$ _____	$3^9 =$ _____

Rewrite each expression as one base and one exponent. Then, find the value.

4. $6^3 \times 6^2 =$ _____ $4^4 \times 4^4 =$ _____ $5^5 \div 5^3 =$ _____

5. $8^9 \div 8^6 =$ _____ $10^2 \times 10^2 =$ _____ $3^8 \div 3^4 =$ _____

6. $7^{10} \div 7^5 =$ _____ $9^2 \times 9^3 =$ _____ $12^{11} \div 12^8 =$ _____

Lesson 3.8 Negative Exponents

When a power includes a negative exponent, express the number as 1 divided by the base and change the exponent to positive.

$$4^{-2} = \frac{1}{4^2}$$
$$= \frac{1}{16}$$
$$= 0.0625$$

To multiply or divide powers with the same base, combine bases, add or subtract the exponents, and then simplify.

$$2^{-3} \times 2^{-2} = 2^{-5} = \frac{1}{2^5} = 0.03125$$
$$2^{-4} \div 2^{-2} = 2^{-2} = \frac{1}{2^2} = 0.25$$

Rewrite each expression with a positive exponent. Then, solve. Round your answer to four decimal places.

	a	b	c
1.	$4^{-3} =$ _____	$6^{-2} =$ _____	$5^{-4} =$ _____
2.	$10^{-4} =$ _____	$2^{-5} =$ _____	$1^{-3} =$ _____

Find each product or quotient. Round your answer to five decimal places.

3. $3^{-4} \times 3^{-2} =$ _____ $6^{-2} \times 6^{-3} =$ _____ $5^{-5} \div 5^{-3} =$ _____

4. $2^{-7} \div 2^{-3} =$ _____ $8^{-2} \times 8^{-2} =$ _____ $7^{-7} \div 7^{-3} =$ _____

5. $4^{-3} \times 4^{-2} =$ _____ $9^{-5} \div 9^{-3} =$ _____ $5^{-3} \div 5^2 =$ _____

6. $2^{-9} \times 2^2 =$ _____ $3^{-7} \times 3^2 =$ _____ $3^{-5} \div 3^2 =$ _____

Lesson 3.9 Finding Angles with Algebra

You can find angles by solving equations. Complementary angles sum to 90 degrees.

$\angle ABD$ and $\angle DBC$ are complementary.

$\angle DBC$ measures $55°$.

What is the measure of $\angle ABD$?

$55° + n = 90°$

$55° + n - 55° = 90° - 55°$

$n = 35°$

$\angle ABD = 35°$

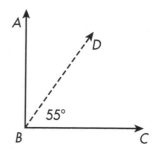

Supplementary angles sum to 180 degrees.

$\angle WXZ$ and $\angle ZXY$ are supplementary.

$\angle WXZ$ measures $150°$.

What is the measure of $\angle ZXY$?

$150° + n = 180°$

$150° + n - 150° = 180° - 150°$

$n = 30°$

$\angle ZXY = 30°$

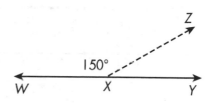

The measure of an angle is two times its supplement. Find the measure of each angle.

$2n + n = 180°$

$3n = 180°$

$\frac{3n}{3} = \frac{180°}{3}$

$n = 60°$

$\angle MKL = 60°$

$2n = 60° \times 2 = 120°$

$\angle JKM = 120°$

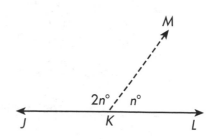

Lesson 3.9 Finding Angles with Algebra

Find the complement of the following angles.

	a	b	c
1.	75° _____	12° _____	33° _____
2.	43° _____	$n°$ _____	$4n°$ _____

Find the supplement of the following angles.

3.	125° _____	92° _____	145° _____
4.	113° _____	$n°$ _____	$5n°$ _____

Find the measure of these angles. Recall that vertical angles are congruent.

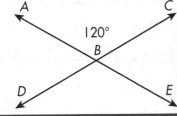

	a	b	c
5.	∠ABD _____	∠DBE _____	∠CBE _____

Write an equation for these problems. Then, solve.

6. An angle is 6 degrees more than its complement. Find the measure of each angle.

_____ The angles measure _____ degrees and _____ degrees.

7. An angle is 3 times the measure of its supplement. Find the measure of each angle.

_____ The angles measure _____ degrees and _____ degrees.

Check What You Learned

Finding Angles with Algebra

Identify the coefficient and the variable in each term below.

| a | b |

1. 61t coefficient_____ variable_____   11 – 3d coefficient_____ variable_____

Write each item as an expression, equation, or inequality. Use n for an unknown number.

2.   19 decreased by a number times 5   15 decreased by a number is less than 7

_____   _____

Underline the operation that should be done first. Then, find the value of the equation.

3. $15 \div 5 \times 7 =$ _____ $6 + 8 \times 4 =$ _____

4. $18 \times 2 \div (6 - 3) =$ _____ $[12 \div (9 - 6)] + 7 =$ _____

Rewrite each expression using the property indicated.

5.   zero: $0 \div 8f =$ _____   associative: $6g + (4h + k)$ _____

6.   identity: $13m + 0 =$ _____   commutative: $2a + 11b =$ _____

Rewrite each expression using the distributive property.

7. $7 \times (n + 6) =$ _____ $9f - 9p =$ _____

8. $11h + 5h =$ _____ $(6 + 7 + 8) \times m =$ _____

Check What You Learned

Finding Angles with Algebra

Find the value of each expression. Round to five decimal places, if needed.

	a	b	c
9.	6^4 _____	$5^3 \times 5^2$ _____	$8^8 \div 8^5$ _____
10.	9^{-3} _____	$3^{-4} \times 3^{-4}$ _____	$7^{-5} \div 7^{-2}$ _____

Find the measure of the complement to each angle.

11.   88° _____   13° _____   29° _____

Find the value of the variable in each equation.

12. $96 - p = 9$ _____ $k + 37 = 54$ _____ $13 \times n = 169$ _____

13. $t \div 5 = 30$ _____ $76 = 4z$ _____ $\frac{72}{r} = 9$ _____

Write an equation for each problem. Then, solve.

14. Ajax Company gave $1,000 total in bonuses to employees. Each employee received $125. How many employees does the company have?

_____ Ajax Company has _____ employees.

15. An angle is 16° more than its supplement. Find the measure of each angle.

_____ The angles measure _____ degrees and _____ degrees.

Check What You Know

Triangles

Calculate the missing angle measures. Indicate whether the triangle is acute, right, or obtuse.

| a | b | c |

1.

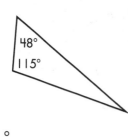

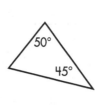

48°
115°

50°
45°

75°

___° _____   ___° _____   ___° ___° _____

Measure each triangle and indicate whether it is equilateral, isosceles, or scalene.

2.

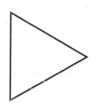

_____   _____   _____

Check that the triangles are proportional. Circle *similar* or *not similar*.

3. $\frac{AB}{DE}$ = _____ = _____

$\frac{BC}{EF}$ = _____ = _____

$\frac{AC}{DF}$ = _____ = _____

34 m B
A   28 m
48 m
        C

51 m E
D   42 m
72 m
        F

similar   not similar

The triangles below are similar. Label the measures of the missing sides.

| a | b |

4.

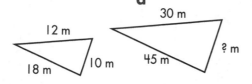

12 m
18 m   10 m

30 m
45 m   ? m

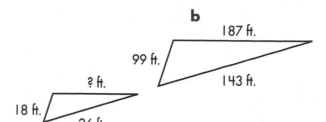

187 ft.
99 ft.   143 ft.

? ft.
18 ft.   26 ft.

Check What You Know

Triangles

Identify the square root of these perfect squares.

a	b	c

5. $\sqrt{225}$ = _____ $\sqrt{64}$ = _____ $\sqrt{484}$ = _____

Estimate the following square roots. Example: $\sqrt{37}$ is between 6 and 7 but closer to 6.

6. $\sqrt{66}$ is between _____ and _____ but closer to _____.

7. $\sqrt{19}$ is between _____ and _____ but closer to _____.

Use the Pythagorean Theorem to determine the length of a, b, or c.

8. If $a = 36$ and $b = 48$, $c = \sqrt{}$ or _____.

9. If $a = 98$ and $c = 170$, $b = \sqrt{}$ or _____.

10. If $b = 77$ and $c = 122$, $a = \sqrt{}$ or _____.

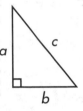

Solve.

11. Campers attached a rope to a pole 12 ft. high. They pulled it tight and staked it to the ground 16 ft. from the pole. How long is the rope? _____

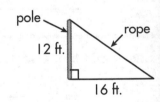

Find the lengths of the missing sides for the similar right triangles.

a	b	c

12. $AB = $ _____ m $DF = $ _____ m $EF = $ _____ m

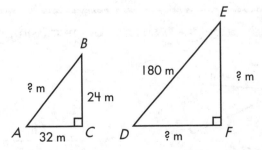

Lesson 4.1 Triangles (by angles)

The sum of all angles in a triangle is always 180°.

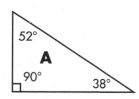
52°
A
90° 38°

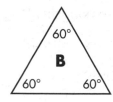
60°
B
60° 60°

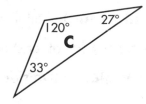
120° 27°
C
33°

$52° + 38° + 90° = 180°$ $60° + 60° + 60° = 180°$ $33° + 120° + 27° = 180°$

A **right triangle** contains 1 right angle, an angle of exactly 90°. Triangle A is a right triangle.

An **acute triangle** contains only acute angles; that is, angles that are less than 90°. Triangle B is an acute triangle.

An **obtuse triangle** contains 1 obtuse angle, an angle greater than 90°. Triangle C is an obtuse triangle.

Label each triangle as acute, right, or obtuse. Check the angles with a protractor, if necessary.

      a   **b**   **c**

1.

_____   _____   _____

Calculate the missing angle measures. Indicate whether the triangle is acute, right, or obtuse.

2.

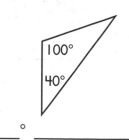
100°
40°

75°
65°

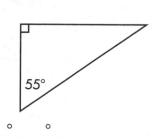
55°

___° _____   ___° _____   ___° ___° _____

Lesson 4.2 Triangles (by sides)

Triangles can be classified by the number of congruent (equal) sides that they have.

In an **equilateral triangle**, all three sides are congruent.

In an **isosceles triangle**, at least two sides are congruent.

In a **scalene triangle**, no two sides are congruent.

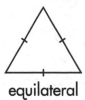
equilateral

isosceles

scalene

Use a ruler to measure each triangle. Write whether it is equilateral, isosceles, or scalene.

a	b	c

1.

_____ _____ _____

2.

_____ _____  _____

Lesson 4.3 Similar Triangles

Two triangles are **similar** if their corresponding (matching) angles are congruent (have the same measure) and the lengths of their corresponding sides are proportional.

The triangles on the right are similar.

All the sides are proportional:

$\frac{AB}{DE} = \frac{12}{8} = \frac{3}{2}$ $\frac{BC}{EF} = \frac{12}{8} = \frac{3}{2}$ $\frac{AC}{DF} = \frac{9}{6} = \frac{3}{2}$

The angle measures are congruent.

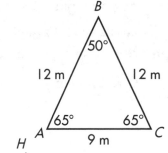

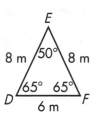

The lower triangles on the right are not similar. The sides are not proportional. They do not all create the same ratio.

The angle measures are not all congruent.

$\frac{GH}{JK} = \frac{4}{3}$ $\frac{HI}{KL} = \frac{6}{5}$ $\frac{GI}{JL} = \frac{5}{5} = \frac{1}{1}$

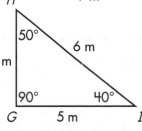

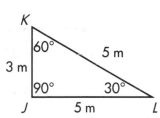

Check that each pair of triangles is proportional. Circle *similar* or *not similar*.

1. $\frac{AB}{DE} =$ _____ = _____

$\frac{BC}{EF} =$ _____ = _____

$\frac{AC}{DF} =$ _____ = _____

similar   not similar

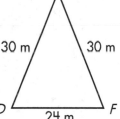

2. $\frac{GH}{JK} =$ _____ = _____

$\frac{HI}{KL} =$ _____ = _____

$\frac{GI}{JL} =$ _____ = _____

similar   not similar

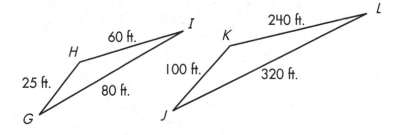

3. $\frac{MN}{PQ} =$ _____ = _____

$\frac{NO}{QR} =$ _____ = _____

$\frac{MO}{PR} =$ _____ = _____

similar   not similar

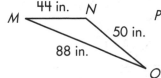

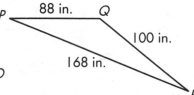

Lesson 4.3 Similar Triangles

When you know that two triangles are similar,
you can use the ratio of the known lengths
of the sides to figure the unknown length.

For example, assume the triangles at right are
similar. What is the length of *EF*? Use a proportion.

$$\frac{AC}{DF} = \frac{BC}{EF} \quad \frac{4}{6} = \frac{12}{n} \quad \text{Cross multiply.}$$
$$4n = 72 \quad n = 18$$

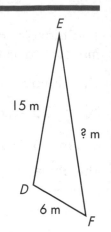
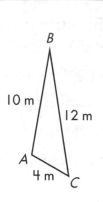

Find the length of the missing side for each pair of similar triangles. Label the side with its length.

a b

1.

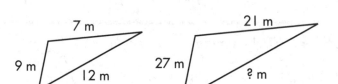

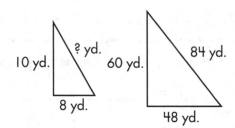

2.

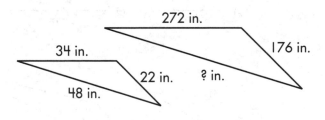

3.

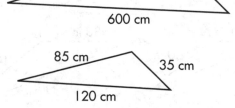

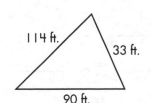

Lesson 4.4 Squares and Square Roots

The **square** of a number is that number times itself. A square is expressed as **6²**, which means 6 x 6 or 6 *squared*. The **square root** of a number is the number that, multiplied by itself, equals that number. The square root of 36 is 6: $\sqrt{36} = 6$.

Not all square roots of numbers are whole numbers like 6. Numbers that have a whole number as their square root are called **perfect squares**.

The square root of any number that is not a perfect square is called a **radical number**. The symbol $\sqrt{}$ is called a **radical sign**. When a number is not a perfect square, you can estimate its square root by determining which perfect squares it comes between.

$\sqrt{50}$ is a little more than 7, because $\sqrt{49}$ is exactly 7. $\sqrt{60}$ is between 7 and 8 but closer to 8, because 60 is closer to 64 than to 49.

If you need help with squares or square roots, refer to the Table of Squares and Square Roots at the back of this book.

Identify the square root of these perfect squares.

	a	b	c
1.	$\sqrt{9} =$ _____	$\sqrt{81} =$ _____	$\sqrt{49} =$ _____
2.	$\sqrt{4} =$ _____	$\sqrt{100} =$ _____	$\sqrt{144} =$ _____
3.	$\sqrt{225} =$ _____	$\sqrt{196} =$ _____	$\sqrt{324} =$ _____

Estimate the following square roots.

4. $\sqrt{8}$ is between _____ and _____ but closer to _____.

5. $\sqrt{80}$ is between _____ and _____ but closer to _____.

6. $\sqrt{140}$ is between _____ and _____ but closer to _____.

7. $\sqrt{88}$ is between _____ and _____ but closer to _____.

8. $\sqrt{250}$ is between _____ and _____ but closer to _____.

Lesson 4.5 The Pythagorean Theorem

The **Pythagorean Theorem** states that the square of the length of the hypotenuse of a right triangle is equal to the sum of the squares of the other two sides. This is true for all right triangles.

In a right triangle, the hypotenuse is the side opposite the right angle. The other two sides are called legs. In this figure, c is the hypotenuse and a and b are the legs.

If a, b, and c are the lengths of the sides of this triangle, $a^2 + b^2 = c^2$.

If $a = 3$ and $b = 4$, what is c?

$a^2 + b^2 = c^2$ $3^2 + 4^2 = c^2$ $9 + 16 = c^2$ $25 = c^2$ $\sqrt{25} = c^2$ $5 = c$

If $a = 4$ and $b = 6$, what is b?

$a^2 + b^2 = c^2$ $4^2 + 6^2 = c^2$ $16 + 36 = c^2$ $52 = c^2$ $\sqrt{52} = c^2$ $\sqrt{52} = c$, about 7.21

Use the Pythagorean Theorem to determine the length of c. Assume that each problem describes a right triangle. Sides a and b are the legs and the hypotenuse is c. If necessary, refer to the Table of Squares and Square Roots at the back of this book.

1. If $a = 7$ and $b = 5$, $c = \sqrt{\rule{2cm}{0pt}}$ or about _____.

2. If $a = 6$ and $b = 8$, $c = \sqrt{\rule{2cm}{0pt}}$ or _____.

3. If $a = 9$ and $b = 4$, $c = \sqrt{\rule{2cm}{0pt}}$ or about _____.

4. If $a = 3$ and $b = 5$, $c = \sqrt{\rule{2cm}{0pt}}$ or about _____.

5. If $a = 2$ and $b = 6$, $c = \sqrt{\rule{2cm}{0pt}}$ or about _____.

6. If $a = 6$ and $b = 9$, $c = \sqrt{\rule{2cm}{0pt}}$ or about _____.

7. If $a = 4$ and $b = 8$, $c = \sqrt{\rule{2cm}{0pt}}$ or about _____.

8. If $a = 3$ and $b = 4$, $c = \sqrt{\rule{2cm}{0pt}}$ or _____.

9. If $a = 2$ and $b = 9$, $c = \sqrt{\rule{2cm}{0pt}}$ or about _____.

10. If $a = 5$ and $b = 9$, $c = \sqrt{\rule{2cm}{0pt}}$ or about _____.

Lesson 4.5 The Pythagorean Theorem

Use the Pythagorean Theorem to find the unknown length of a side of a right triangle when the other two lengths are known.

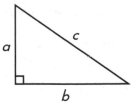

If $a = 12$ m and $c = 13$ m, what is b?

$a^2 + b^2 = c^2$ $12^2 + b^2 = 13^2$

$144 + b^2 = 169$

$144 + b^2 - 144 = 169 - 144$

$b^2 = 25$ $b = \sqrt{25}$ $b = 5$ m

If $b = 15$ ft. and $c = 17$ ft., what is a?

$a^2 + b^2 = c^2$ $a^2 + 15^2 = 17^2$

$a^2 + 225 = 289$

$a^2 + 225 - 225 = 289 - 225$

$a^2 = 64$ $a = \sqrt{64}$ $a = 8$ ft.

Assume that each problem describes a right triangle. Use the Pythagorean Theorem to find the unknown lengths. If necessary, refer to the Table of Squares and Square Roots at the back of this book.

1. If $a = 8$ and $c = 10$, $b = \sqrt{\underline{\hspace{2cm}}}$ or _____.

2. If $a = 12$ and $c = 16$, $b = \sqrt{\underline{\hspace{2cm}}}$ or _____.

3. If $b = 18$ and $c = 22$, $a = \sqrt{\underline{\hspace{2cm}}}$ or _____.

4. If $b = 8$ and $c = 14$, $a = \sqrt{\underline{\hspace{2cm}}}$ or _____.

5. If $a = 4$ and $c = 8$, $b = \sqrt{\underline{\hspace{2cm}}}$ or _____.

6. Alicia attached a support wire to the top of a flagpole. The wire was 65 ft. long, and she staked the wire 45 ft. from the pole. How tall was the flagpole?

   The flagpole was _____ feet tall.

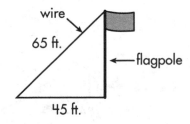

7. Tom is building a ramp to the back entrance of his house. The ramp will be attached to the house 12 ft. above the ground. He wants the end of the ramp to be 26 ft. from the house. What will be the length of the ramp?

   The ramp will be _____ feet long.

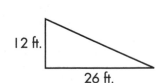

Lesson 4.6 The Pythagorean Theorem and Similar Right Triangles

Use the Pythagorean Theorem and ratios of similar triangles to find the unknown lengths of sides.

First, find the length of *AB*.

$$a^2 + b^2 = c^2 \qquad a^2 + 12^2 = 15^2 \qquad a^2 + 144 = 225$$

$$a^2 + 144 - 144 = 225 - 144 \qquad a^2 = 81 \quad a = 9 \text{ ft.}$$

Use ratios to find the unknown lengths of *EF* and *DF*.

$$\frac{AB}{DE} = \frac{BC}{EF} \qquad \frac{9}{15} = \frac{12}{n}$$

$$9n = 180 \quad n = 20$$

The length of *EF* is 20 ft.

$$\frac{AB}{DE} = \frac{AC}{DF} \qquad \frac{9}{15} = \frac{15}{n}$$

$$9n = 225 \quad n = 25$$

The length of *DF* is 25 ft.

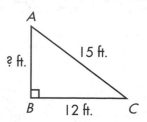
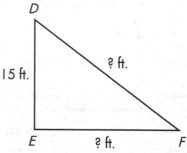

Find the lengths of the missing sides for each pair of similar right triangles.

	a	**b**	**c**
1.	MN = _____ m	QR = _____ m	PR = _____ m
2.	AB = _____ ft.	EF = _____ ft.	DF = _____ ft.
3.	KL = _____ m	HJ = _____ m	JI = _____ m

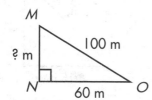

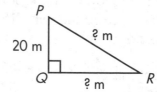

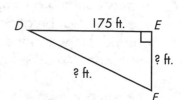

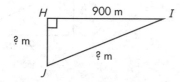

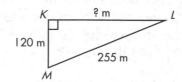

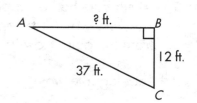

NAME _____

Check What You Learned

Triangles

Calculate the missing angle measures. Indicate whether the triangle is acute, right, or obtuse.

1.

a
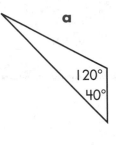
120°
40°

____° _____

b
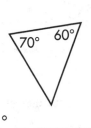
70° 60°

____° _____

c
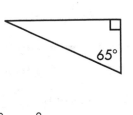
65°

____° ____° _____

Measure each triangle and indicate whether it is equilateral, isosceles, or scalene.

2.

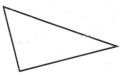

_____ _____ _____

Check that the triangles are proportional. Circle *similar* or *not similar*.

3. $\frac{AB}{DE} =$ _____ = _____

$\frac{BC}{EF} =$ _____ = _____

$\frac{AC}{DF} =$ _____ = _____

similar   not similar

38 m
A   C
14 m   32 m
B

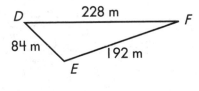
D   228 m   F
84 m   192 m
E

The triangles below are similar. Label the measures of the missing sides.

a

4.

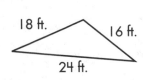
18 ft.   16 ft.
24 ft.

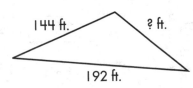
144 ft.   ? ft.
192 ft.

b

26 m
? m

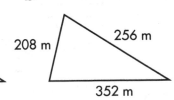
256 m
208 m
352 m

Check What You Learned

Triangles

Identify the square root of these perfect squares.

a	**b**	**c**
5. $\sqrt{121}$ = _____	$\sqrt{256}$ = _____	$\sqrt{144}$ = _____

Estimate the following square roots.

6. $\sqrt{86}$ is between _____ and _____ but closer to _____.

Use the Pythagorean Theorem to determine the length of a, b, or c.

7. If a = 22 and b = 27, c = $\sqrt{}$ or _____.

8. If a = 48 and c = 92, b = $\sqrt{}$ or _____.

9. If b = 184 and c = 232, a = $\sqrt{}$ or _____.

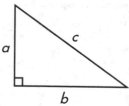

Solve.

10. Paul is building a deck within a corner of his house that measures 25 by 30 feet. How long will the deck extend from one corner of his house to the other, rounded to the nearest foot?

The deck will be _____ feet.

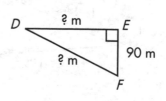

Find the lengths of the missing sides for the similar right triangles.

a	**b**	**c**
11. BC = _____ m	DE = _____ m	DF = _____ m

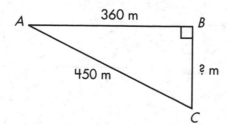
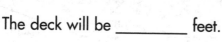

Mid-Test Chapters 1–4

Use the figure to complete the following problems.

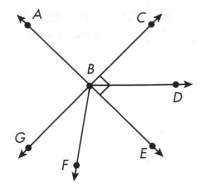

1. Is *BF* a line, a line segment, or a ray? _____

2. Name two sets of collinear points. _____, _____

3. Is ∠*GBF* an acute angle, an obtuse angle, or a right angle? _____

4. Name an angle that is vertical to ∠*ABG*. _____

5. Name an angle that is complementary to ∠*EBF*. _____

6. ∠*CBE* is 90°. $\overrightarrow{BD}$ bisects ∠*CBE*. What is the angle measure of ∠*DBE*? _____

7. Name the two angles that are supplementary to ∠*ABC*. _____

Use the figure to complete the following problems.

8. Name the alternate interior angles.

   ∠_____/∠_____   ∠_____/∠_____

9. Name the alternate exterior angles.

   ∠_____/∠_____   ∠_____/∠_____

10. ∠5 and ∠6 are adjacent. If ∠6 is 70°, what is the measure of ∠5? _____

11. Name the transversal of $\overleftrightarrow{HJ}$ and $\overleftrightarrow{KM}$. _____

12. Name an adjacent angle to ∠3. _____

Mid-Test Chapters 1–4

Cross-multiply to see if the ratios form a true proportion, or equality of ratios. Show your work. Write a *T* next to proportions that are true.

	a	**b**	**c**

13. $\frac{3}{6} = \frac{8}{2}$ _____ $\frac{11}{22} = \frac{1}{2}$ _____ $\frac{3}{2} = 12:8$ _____

14.   1 to 5 = 7 to 35 _____   6 to 7 = 12 to 14 _____ $\frac{22}{16} = \frac{7}{5}$ _____

Solve for *n* in each proportion.

15.   2 to 5 = 10 to *n* _____ $\frac{8}{n} = \frac{64}{3}$ _____ $\frac{8}{9} = \frac{n}{6}$ _____

16.   7 to 2 = *n* to 14 _____   9:3 = 18:*n* _____ $\frac{2}{3} = \frac{n}{48}$ _____

Write a proportion for each problem. Then, solve the problem.

17.   Members of the school band are selling apple pies at $14 per pie. How many pies must they sell in order to make $700?

_____ The band members must sell _____ pies.

18.   Maria wants to make a scale drawing of her bedroom. The scale is 2 cm = 1 foot. If her bedroom is 14 feet long by 12 feet wide, what is the length and width of her scale drawing?

_____ The length is _____ cm, and the width is _____ cm.

19.   The new city hall uses the golden ratio in its design. If the width of the new building is 530 m, what is the length?

_____ The length is _____ m.

Mid-Test Chapters 1–4

Rewrite each expression using the property indicated.

20. commutative: $r + 2s =$ _____   identity: $1 \times 12w =$ _____

21. associative: $6g + (4h + k)$ _____   distributive: $(10 - 5) \times p =$ _____

22. distributive: $4x + 4z =$ _____   zero: $0 \times (9 + 6x) =$ _____

Find the value of the variable in each equation.

	a	b	c

23. $23 = a + 7$ _____ $6b = 108$ _____ $2 \times 7n = 42$ _____

Find the value of each expression.

24. 3^{-2} _____ $5^9 \div 5^6$ _____ $4^4 \times 2^{-3}$ _____

Find the measure of the supplement to each angle.

25. $135°$ _____ $45°$ _____ $s°$ _____

Write an equation for the problem. Then, solve.

26. An angle is 25 degrees less than its complement. Find the measure of each angle.

_____ The angles measure _____ degrees and _____ degrees.

Mid-Test Chapters 1–4

Check whether the triangles are proportional.
Circle similar or not similar.

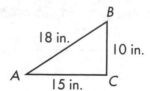 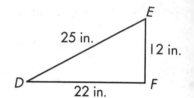

27. $\frac{AB}{DE}$ = _____ = _____

$\frac{BC}{EF}$ = _____ = _____

$\frac{AC}{DF}$ = _____ = _____

similar   not similar

Use the Pythagorean Theorem to determine the length of a, b, or c.

28. If $a = 13$ and $c = 15$, $b = \sqrt{\underline{\hspace{1cm}}}$ or _____.

29. If $a = 8$ and $b = 6$, $c = \sqrt{\underline{\hspace{1cm}}}$ or _____.

30. If $b = 121$ and $c = 196$, $a = \sqrt{\underline{\hspace{1cm}}}$ or _____.

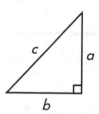

Solve.

31. Miranda's sailboat needs a new sail. If the sail is 7 feet wide and measures 12 feet long, how tall must the mast be?

_____ The mast must be _____ feet.

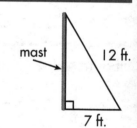

Find the lengths of the missing sides for the similar right triangles.

       a   **b**   **c**

32. AB = _____ cm   DE = _____ cm   EF = _____ cm

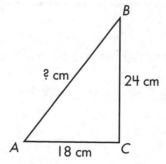 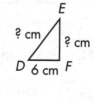

Check What You Know

Polygons

Write the name for each regular polygon. Find the sum of all its angles and the measure of one angle.

1.

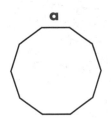 **a**

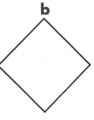 **b**

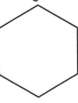 **c**

_____

sum of angles: _____°

one angle: _____°

_____

sum of angles: _____°

one angle: _____°

_____

sum of angles: _____°

one angle: _____°

2.

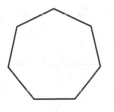

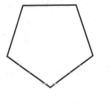

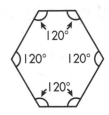

_____

sum of angles: _____°

one angle: _____°

_____

sum of angles: _____°

one angle: _____°

_____

sum of angles: _____°

one angle: _____°

Write the name for each polygon. Label it as equiangular, equilateral, or regular.

3.

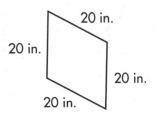

20 in.
20 in.
20 in.
20 in.

25 cm 60° 25 cm
60° 60°
25 cm

120°
120° 120°
120°

_____

_____

_____

_____

_____

_____

NAME _____

Check What You Know

Polygons

Use the figures to complete the statements and answer the questions.

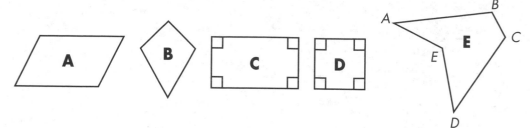

4. Figure A is a _____. Its _____ sides are parallel and congruent.

5. There are no _____ sides in Figure B. It is a _____.

6. Figure C is a _____ which is a type of _____.

7. Figure D is a _____. It differs from figure C in that all four of its sides are _____.

8. Name the nonconsecutive vertices in figure E. _____

9. Is figure E a convex or concave polygon? _____

For each pair of figures, write ratios to determine if the sides are proportional. Then, write *similar* or *not similar*.

a

b

10.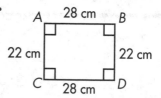

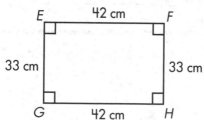

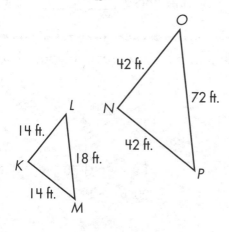

_____   _____

Lesson 5.1 Polygons

The **polygon** is a closed plane figure made up of straight lines. See the table at right. Polygons are named according to the number of their sides. A **triangle** has 3 sides and a **quadrilateral** has 4 sides.

If all the sides of a polygon are congruent (the same length), it is **equilateral**. If all its angles are congruent (the same measure), it is **equiangular**. If a polygon is both equilateral and equiangular, it is a **regular polygon**.

Prefix	Name	Sides
tri-	triangle	3
quadri-	quadrilateral	4
penta-	pentagon	5
hexa-	hexagon	6
hepta-	heptagon	7
octa-	octagon	8
nona-	nonagon	9
deca-	decagon	10

Find the sum of the measures of the interior angles of a polygon with the formula $(n - 2)180$ degrees, where n is the number of sides. To get the interior measure of one angle of the regular polygon, divide the sum by the number of sides. The following example is for a pentagon.

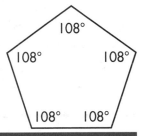

$(n - 2)180°$ $(5 - 2)180 = 540°$ $540° ÷ 5 = 108°$

Write the name for each regular polygon. Then, find the sum of the measures of the interior angles and the measure of one angle.

| a | b | c |

1.

_____   _____   _____

sum of angles: _____°   sum of angles: _____°   sum of angles: _____°

one angle:_____°   one angle: _____°   one angle: _____°

Name each polygon and label it as equiangular, equilateral, or regular.

2.

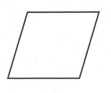   

_____   _____   _____

_____   _____   _____

Lesson 5.1 Polygons

A **vertex** is the point where any two sides of a polygon meet. In figure A, the sides AB and BC meet at the vertex B. Since the sides AB and BC share a vertex, they are **consecutive sides**.

The two endpoints of a side, such as vertex B and vertex C, are called **consecutive vertices**. The dashed lines in figure A are diagonals. A **diagonal** is a line segment drawn between any two **nonconsecutive vertices** such as B, D or A, C.

A polygon is either convex or concave. It is **convex** if all the interior angles are less than 180° and all the diagonals appear in the interior of the figure. It is **concave** if at least one interior angle is greater than 180° and at least one diagonal falls outside the figure. In the concave polygon (figure B), the diagonal HJ is outside the figure.

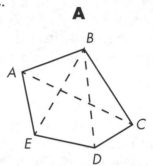
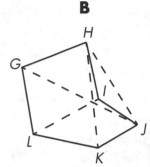

Convex Polygon   **Concave Polygon**

Name all pairs of nonconsecutive vertices in each polygon. Then, draw all the diagonals. Label each polygon as concave or convex.

a   **b**

1.

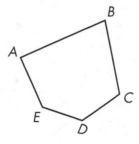

nonconsecutive vertices: _____

concave or convex _____

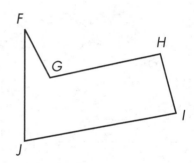

nonconsecutive vertices: _____

concave or convex _____

2.

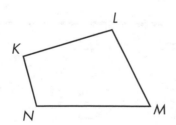

nonconsecutive vertices: _____

concave or convex _____

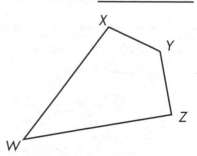

nonconsecutive vertices: _____

concave or convex _____

Lesson 5.2 Quadrilaterals

A **quadrilateral** is a closed figure with 4 sides. It has 4 vertices. The sum of the angle measures of a quadrilateral is 360°.

A **parallelogram** is a quadrilateral whose opposite sides are parallel and congruent.

A **rectangle** is a parallelogram with four right angles.

A **square** has four right angles and four congruent sides. (A square is a special kind of rectangle and a special kind of rhombus.)

A **rhombus** is a parallelogram with four congruent sides. Opposite sides are parallel and opposite angles are equal.

A **trapezoid** is a quadrilateral with only one pair of parallel sides, called *bases*. Nonparallel sides are called *legs*.

A **kite** has two pairs of congruent adjacent sides but no parallel sides.

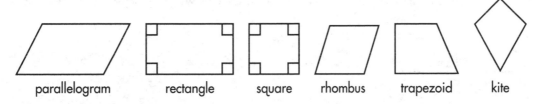

parallelogram   rectangle   square   rhombus   trapezoid   kite

Use the figures to answer each question.

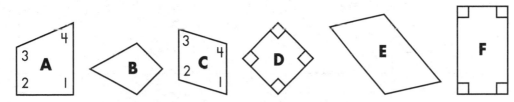

1. Write three names for figure D. _____ _____ _____

2. Write two names for figure F. _____ _____

3. Describe a difference between figures D and F. _____

4. What is the name for figure A? _____

5. In figure A, ∠1 and ∠2 are 90° and ∠3 is 115°. What is the measure of ∠4? _____°

6. Write two names for figure C. _____ _____

7. In figure C, if ∠1 is 70°, what is the measure of ∠3? _____°

8. Name figure B. _____

Lesson 5.3 Similar Figures

Two figures are **similar** if their corresponding angles are congruent and the lengths of their corresponding sides are proportional. Write a ratio to determine if the sides are proportional.

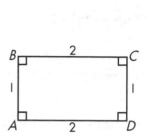
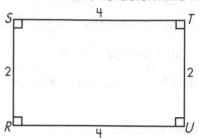
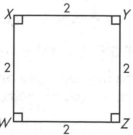

$\frac{AB}{RS} = \frac{BC}{ST}$ $\frac{1}{2} = \frac{2}{4}$ Similar

$\frac{AB}{WX} = \frac{BC}{XY}$ $\frac{1}{2} \neq \frac{2}{2}$ Not Similar

For each pair of figures, write ratios to determine if the sides are proportional. Then, write *similar* or *not similar*. Note: In the figures, the angle marks indicate which angles are congruent.

a	b

1.

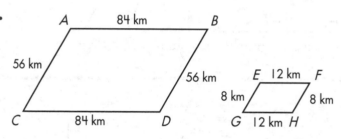
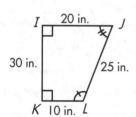
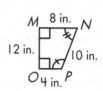

_____   _____

2.

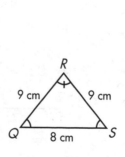
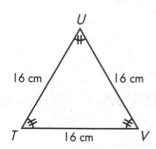
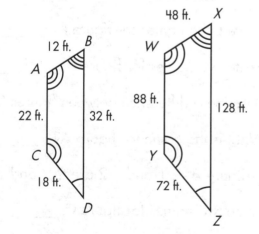

_____   _____

Check What You Learned

Polygons

Write the name for each regular polygon. Find the sum of all its angles and the measure of one angle.

| a | b | c |

1.

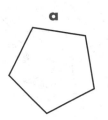      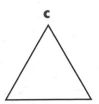

_____

sum of angles: _____°

one angle: _____°

_____

sum of angles: _____°

one angle: _____°

_____

sum of angles: _____°

one angle: _____°

2.

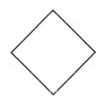      

_____

sum of angles: _____°

one angle: _____°

_____

sum of angles: _____°

one angle: _____°

_____

sum of angles: _____°

one angle: _____°

Write the name for each polygon. Label it as equiangular, equilateral, or regular.

3.

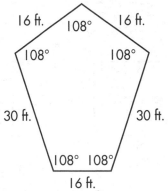   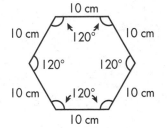   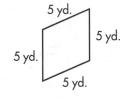

_____

_____

_____

_____

_____

_____

Check What You Learned

Polygons

Use the figures to complete the statements and answer the questions.

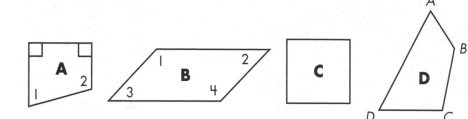

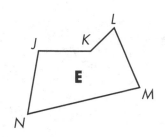

4. Figure A is a _____. Its parallel sides are called _____. Its nonparallel sides are called _____.

5. The sum of the interior angles of a quadrilateral is _____°. There are two right angles in figure A, and ∠2 is 110°. So, the measure of ∠1 is _____°.

6. Figure B is a _____. In figure B, ∠1 and ∠4 are congruent. ∠1 measures 128°, so ∠4 measures _____°.

7. Figure C is a square. Each interior angle measures _____°.

8. On the lines below, name all pairs of nonconsecutive vertices in figures D and E.

   Figure D: _____ Figure E: _____.

9. Which figure is concave, figure D or figure E? _____.

For each pair of figures, write ratios to determine if the sides are proportional. Then, write *similar* or *not similar*.

10.

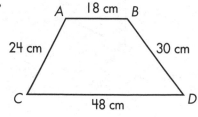

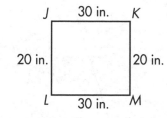

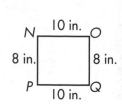

_____   _____

Check What You Know

The Coordinate Plane

Add or subtract the following integers.

	a	**b**	**c**
1.	$2 - 18 =$ _____	$-7 - (-7) =$ _____	$-15 + (-6) =$ _____
2.	$-3 - (-9) =$ _____	$2 + 3 =$ _____	$7 - 18 =$ _____
3.	$10 + 4 =$ _____	$-17 + (-3) =$ _____	$-5 + 14 =$ _____
4.	$12 + (-5) =$ _____	$4 - 9 =$ _____	$-2 + 2 =$ _____

Use the grid to name a point for each ordered pair.

5. $(8, 4)$ _____ $(7, 2)$ _____

6. $(9, 1)$ _____ $(9, 9)$ _____

Using the same grid, name the ordered pair for each point.

7. $C ($____, ____$)$ $A ($____, ____$)$

8. $F ($____, ____$)$ $H ($____, ____$)$

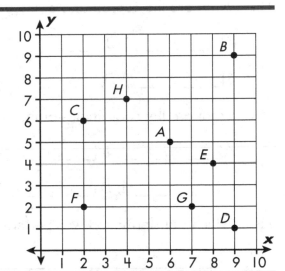

Plot the points shown on the grid. Label the points.

	a	**b**
9.	$M(4, 4)$	$N(-6, -6)$
10.	$O(-4, 6)$	$P(5, -4)$
11.	$Q(-3, -3)$	$R(9, 2)$

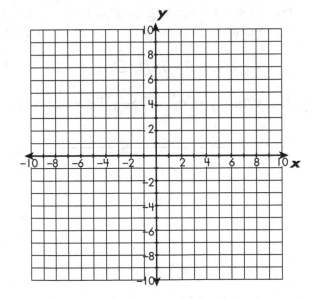

NAME _____

Check What You Know

The Coordinate Plane

12. Is the transformation shown in the grid a translation, rotation, reflection, or dilation?

_____

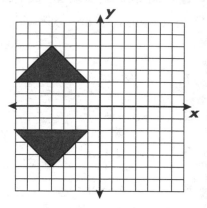

13. What are the coordinates of the preimage?

A(____, ____), B(____, ____),

C(____, ____), D(____, ____)

14. What are the coordinates of the image?

A'(____, ____), B'(____, ____),

C'(____, ____), D'(____, ____)

15. Which transformation was performed on this figure?

_____

16. Plot the following coordinates on the grid at right and connect the points by straight lines.

A(–8, 5), B(–6, 7), C(–4, 5), D(–4, 2), E(–8, 2)

17. What type of polygon did you draw?

_____

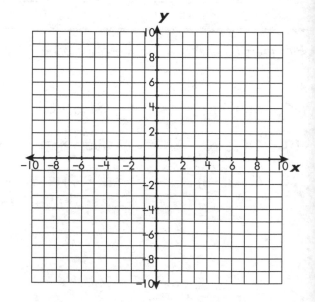

Lesson 6.1 Working with Integers

Integers are the set of whole numbers and their opposites. **Positive integers** are greater than zero. **Negative integers** are less than zero, and they are always less than positive integers.

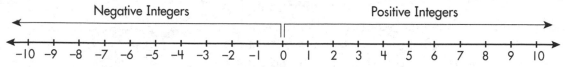

The sum of two positive integers is a positive integer. $4 + 3 = 7$

The sum of two negative integers is a negative integer. $-4 + (-3) = -7$

To find the sum of a positive and negative integer, first find their absolute values. **Absolute value** is the distance (in units) that a number is from 0 expressed as a positive quantity. It is written as $|x|$.

To add -4 and 3, find the absolute values.

$|-4| = 4$

$|3| = 3$

$4 - 3 = -1$

Then, subtract the lesser number from the greater number. The sum has the same sign as the integer with the larger absolute value.

Since 4 is negative, the answer is negative.

$5 - 7 = 5 + (-7) = -2$

Add or subtract.

	a	**b**	**c**
I.	$6 + 3 =$ _____	$10 + (-2) =$ _____	$-5 + 13 =$ _____
2.	$2 - 9 =$ _____	$-3 - 6 =$ _____	$7 - (-5) =$ _____
3.	$-35 - 0 =$ _____	$-2 + (-7) =$ _____	$-13 + (-7) =$ _____
4.	$7 - 19 =$ _____	$11 + (-33) =$ _____	$12 - 23 =$ _____
5.	$-4 + 4 =$ _____	$-1 + 3 =$ _____	$9 + (-8) =$ _____
6.	$-5 + (-5) =$ _____	$10 - (-1) =$ _____	$-13 - 6 =$ _____

Lesson 6.2 Plotting Ordered Pairs

The position of any point on a grid can be described by an **ordered pair** of numbers. The two numbers are named in order: (x, y). Point A on the grid at the right is named by the ordered pair (3, 2). It is located at 3 on the horizontal scale (x) and 2 on the vertical scale (y). The number on the horizontal scale is always named first in an ordered pair. Point B is named by the ordered pair (7, 3).

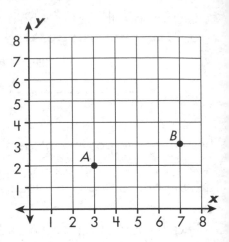

Use Grid 1 to name the point or ordered pair.

1. (7, 2) _____   (3, 4) _____

2. (3, 6) _____   (9, 6) _____

3. L (____ , ____)   C (____ , ____)

4. J (____ , ____)   I (____ , ____)

5. F (____ , ____)   K (____ , ____)

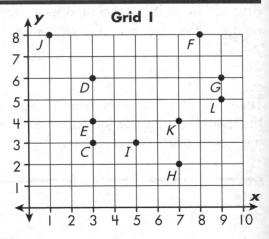

Plot the four points on Grid 2. Label each point.

6. (1, 5) _____   (5, 3) _____

7. (7, 4) _____   (2, 2) _____

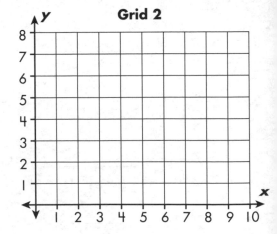

Lesson 6.2 Plotting Ordered Pairs

A **coordinate plane** is formed by two intersecting number lines. The **x-axis** is the horizontal line. The **y-axis** is the vertical line. The **origin** is located at the ordered pair (0, 0). The coordinate plane is divided into four quadrants, which are named in counterclockwise order, as shown on the right.

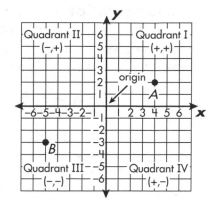

As you already learned, ordered pairs are listed as (x, y). These two numbers show the distance from the ordered pair to the origin, along the x- and y-axes.

On the right, Point A is located at (4, 2). Point B is located at (−5, −3).

Plot each ordered pair on Grid 1.

Grid 1

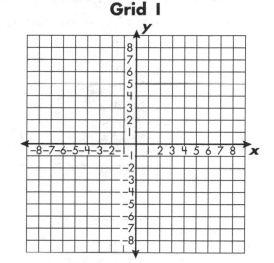

1. A(4, 5)   B(−4, −3)

2. C(2, −3)   D(−3, 2)

3. E(7, 1)   F(−7, 8)

4. G(6, −4)   H(−6, −7)

5. I(1, 1)   J(4, −7)

Write where each lettered point is located on Grid 2.

Grid 2

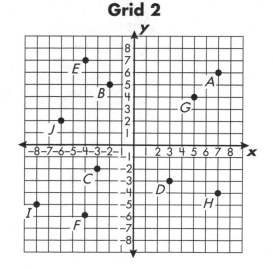

6. A(____, ____)   B(____, ____)

7. C(____, ____)   D(____, ____)

8. E(____, ____)   F(____, ____)

9. G(____, ____)   H(____, ____)

10. I(____, ____)   J(____, ____)

Lesson 6.3 Transformations

A **transformation** is a change of the position or size of an image. In a **translation**, an image slides in any direction. In a **rotation**, an image is turned about a point. In a **reflection**, an image is flipped over a line. In a **dilation**, an image is enlarged or reduced. One way to view an image and its transformation is to graph it on a coordinate plane, as shown below.

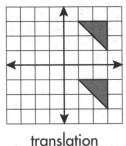
translation

rotation

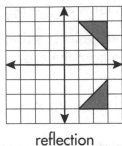
reflection

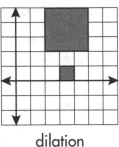
dilation

Write whether each transformation is a translation, rotation, reflection, or dilation.

	a	b	c

1.

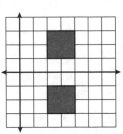

_____   _____   _____

2.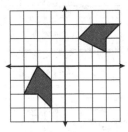

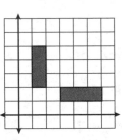

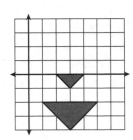

_____   _____   _____

3.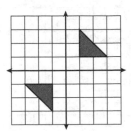

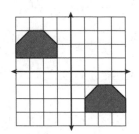

_____   _____   _____

Lesson 6.3 Transformations

Graphing figures on a coordinate plane helps show how they are translated. The original figure is called a **preimage**. The translated figure is called the **image**. Read the numbers on the x-axis and y-axis to determine the location of the figure.

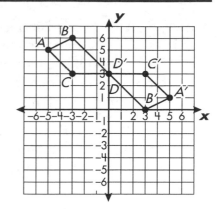

This figure has been rotated 180° about one point of the figure. As a result, the preimage and the image share a point. The 4 corners of the preimage are points A, B, C, and D. The 4 corners of the image are points A', B', C', and D'.

The coordinates of the preimage are A(–5, 5), B(–3, 6), C(–3, 3), D(0,3.)

The coordinates of the image are: A'(5, 1), B'(3, 0), C'(3, 3), and D' (0, 3)

---

1. What are the coordinates of the preimage?

    A(_____), B(_____), C(_____)

2. What are the coordinates of the image?

    A'(_____), B'(_____), C'(_____)

3. What transformation was performed on the figure?

    _____

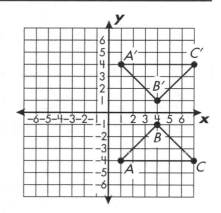

---

4. What are the coordinates of the preimage?

    A(_____), B(_____), C(_____), D(_____)

5. Draw a transformed image with the following coordinates.

    A'(3, 4), B'(5, 3), C'(3, 1), D'(1, 2)

6. What transformation was performed on the figure?

    _____

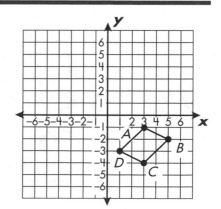

Lesson 6.4 Drawing Shapes

A **polygon** is a closed shape created by straight lines. The **vertices** of a polygon are the points where the lines intersect. These vertices can be described by coordinates and plotted on a coordinate plane. When the points are connected by straight lines, they form a polygon.

The points A(–6, 3), B(–3, 6), and C(–3, 1) are plotted on a coordinate plane. When the points are connected with straight lines, they form a triangle, a type of polygon.

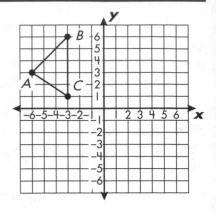

Plot the points on the coordinate plane and connect the points with straight lines.

1. A(–2, 3), B(2, 3), C(–4, –2), D(4, –2)

Which type of polygon did you draw?

_____

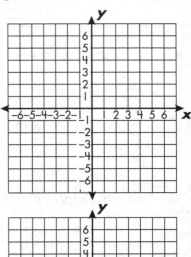

2. E(1, –3), F(5, –1), G(5, –5), H(4, –3)

Which type of polygon did you draw?

_____

3. I(–3, 5), J(4, 5), K(1, 2), L(–6, 2)

Which type of polygon did you draw?

_____

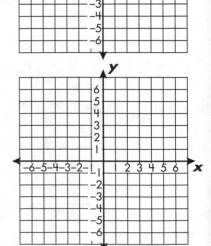

NAME _____

Check What You Learned

The Coordinate Plane

Add or subtract the following integers.

	a	b	c
1.	5 + 9 = _____	12 − 15 = _____	−6 + (−20) = _____
2.	17 − 23 = _____	−8 − (−4) = _____	7 − 18 = _____
3.	13 + 2 = _____	11 − (−6) = _____	−3 + (−6) = _____
4.	−5 + 1 = _____	32 − (−9) = _____	6 − 4 = _____

Use the grid to name a point for each ordered pair.

5.   (8, 7) _____   (4, 3) _____

6.   (1, 7) _____   (3, 5) _____

Using the same grid, name the ordered pair for each point.

7.   A(____, ____)   H(____, ____)

8.   F(____, ____)   D(____, ____)

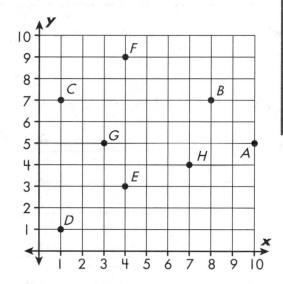

Plot the points shown on the grid. Label the points.

	a	b
9.	M(−3, −4)	N(9, −6)
10.	O(−5, 7)	P(7, −2)
11.	Q(−7, 2)	R(8, 7)

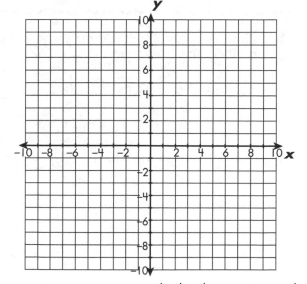

Check What You Learned

The Coordinate Plane

12. Is the transformation shown in the grid a translation, rotation, reflection, or dilation? _____

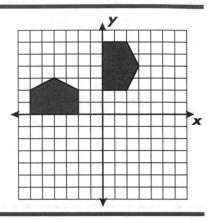

13. Which transformation was performed on this figure?

_____

14. What are the coordinates of the preimage?

A(_____, _____), B(_____, _____),

C(_____, _____), D(_____, _____)

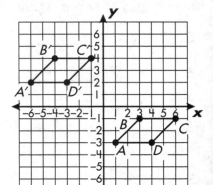

15. What are the coordinates of the image?

A'(_____, _____), B'(_____, _____),

C'(_____, _____), D'(_____, _____)

16. Plot the following coordinates on the grid and connect the points by straight lines.

A(3, 8), B(6, 8), C(8, 6), D(8, 3),

E(6, 1), F(3, 1), G(1, 3), H(1, 6)

17. What type of polygon did you draw?

_____

Check What You Know

NAME _____

Circles and Solid Figures

Use the circle to answer the questions.

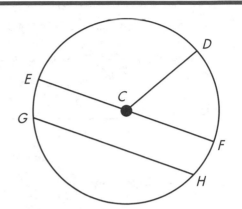

1. Name the circle. _____

2. Name the origin. _____

3. Name a radius. _____

4. Name a chord. _____

5. Name the diameter. _____

Find the circumference of each circle. Use 3.14 for π.

6.

28 in.

12 cm

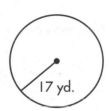
17 yd.

_____ inches   _____ centimeters   _____ yards

Match each term with its picture.

7. cone _____

8. rectangular solid _____

9. triangular pyramid _____

10. cube _____

11. square pyramid _____

12. cylinder _____

13. triangular solid _____

 A
 B
 C
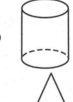 D
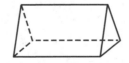 E
 F
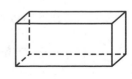 G

NAME _____

Check What You Know

Circles and Solid Figures

Answer each question. Use 3.14 for π.

14. Is a line segment with one endpoint at the origin and the other endpoint on the circle called a *chord* or a *radius*?

It is called a _____.

15. How is a circle named?

It is named by its _____.

16. If the circumference of a circle is 15.7 feet, what is the diameter? What is the radius?

The diameter is _____ feet. The radius is _____ feet.

17. On a basketball court, the diameter of the center circle is 12 feet. What is the circle's circumference?

The circle's circumference is _____ feet.

18. Alex holds a solid figure that has 2 circular bases. Is the figure a cone or a cylinder?

The solid figure is a _____.

19. A cube has 6 faces. Are the faces rectangular or square?

The cube's faces are _____.

Lesson 7.1 Circles

A **circle** is a set of points that are all the same distance from a given point, called the center or the **origin**. A circle is named by its origin.

A **radius** of a circle is a line segment with one endpoint at the origin and the other endpoint on the circle.

A **chord** is a line segment with both endpoints on the circle.

A **diameter** is a chord that passes through the origin of the circle.

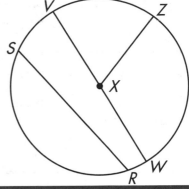

Name a radius, chord, and diameter of circle X.

  radius: $\overline{XZ}$, $\overline{XV}$, or $\overline{XW}$ chord: $\overline{VW}$ or $\overline{SR}$ diameter: $\overline{VW}$

Identify each line segment as a radius, chord, or diameter.

	a	**b**	**c**

1.

_____   _____   _____

Use the figure at the right to answer the questions.

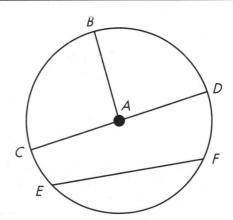

2. Name the circle. _____

3. Name the origin. _____

4. Name a radius. _____

5. Name a chord. _____

6. Name the diameter. _____

7. Draw a circle L, with radius $\overline{LM}$, diameter $\overline{NO}$, and chord $\overline{RS}$.

Lesson 7.2 Circumference of a Circle

The perimeter of a circle is called the **circumference**.

The relationship between the circumference (C) and the diameter (d) is $C \div d = \pi$. Pi (π) is approximately $3\frac{1}{7}$ or 3.14.

To find the circumference, diameter, or radius of a circle, use the formulas $C = \pi \times d$ or $C = 2 \times \pi \times r$.

If the diameter of a circle is 4 cm, the circumference is 4π cm, or about 12.56 cm.

If the radius of a circle is 5 cm, the circumference is $2\pi5$ cm, or about 31.4 cm.

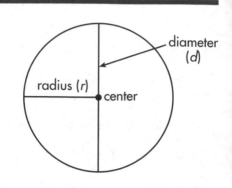

Complete the table below. Use 3.14 for π. If necessary, round answers to the nearest hundredth.

	a Diameter	b Radius	c Circumference
1.	_____ ft.	_____ ft.	9.42 ft.
2.	37 cm	_____ cm	_____ cm
3.	_____ yd.	12 yd.	_____ yd.
4.	4.5 mm	_____ mm	_____ mm
5.	_____ km	_____ km	31.4 km
6.	24.2 in.	_____ in.	_____ in.
7.	_____ mi.	5.25 mi.	_____ mi.
8.	_____ cm	_____ cm	4.71 cm
9.	_____ ft.	4.8 ft.	_____ ft.

Lesson 7.3 Solid Figures

A **solid figure** is a three-dimensional figure. A **face** is a flat surface of a solid figure. An **edge** is the intersection of two faces. A **vertex** is a point where three or more faces meet. A **base** is a face on which the solid figure rests.

A **cube** has
6 square faces.

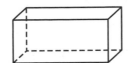

A **rectangular solid** has
6 rectangular faces.

A **triangular solid** has
2 triangular faces and
3 rectangular faces.

A **cone** has
a circular base
and 1 vertex.

A **triangular pyramid** has
4 triangular faces.

A **square pyramid** has
1 square base and
4 triangular faces.

A **cylinder** has
2 circular bases.

Name each figure shown at the right.

1. A _____   4. D _____

2. B _____   5. E _____

3. C _____   6. F _____

For the figures above, indicate the number of faces and whether they are square, rectangular, triangular, or circular.

	Number of Faces	Type(s) of Face(s)
7.	A _____	_____
8.	B _____	_____
9.	C _____	_____
10.	D _____	_____
11.	E _____	_____
12.	F _____	_____ _____

Lesson 7.4 Problem Solving

Answer each question. Use 3.14 for π. If necessary, round answers to the nearest hundredth.

1. Maurice says that a line segment with both endpoints on a circle is called a *radius*. Shaylin says that it is called a *chord*. Who is correct?

_____ is correct.

2. What is the name of a chord that passes through the origin of a circle?

The name of this chord is a _____.

3. If the circumference of a circle is 18.84 inches, what is the diameter? What is the radius?

The diameter is _____ inches. The radius is _____ inches.

4. June draws a chalk circle on the playground that is 2 feet in diameter. What is the circle's circumference?

The circle's circumference is _____ feet.

5. Padma is holding a solid figure that has 6 square faces. Which kind of solid figure is this?

The solid figure is a _____.

6. What is the name of a solid figure with 2 circular bases?

The name of this solid figure is a _____.

Check What You Learned

Circles and Solid Figures

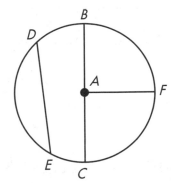

Use the circle to answer the questions.

1. What is A? _____

2. What is $\overline{BC}$? _____

3. What is $\overline{AF}$? _____

4. What is $\overline{DE}$? _____

5. What is the circle's name? _____

Fill in the blanks below. Use 3.14 for π.

6.

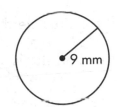

radius: _____mi.   circumference: _____ft.   diameter:_____mm

Match each term with its description. Each description is used only once.

7. _____ cylinder

8. _____ triangular pyramid

9. _____ square pyramid

10. _____ cone

11. _____ rectangular solid

12. _____ triangular solid

13. _____ cube

A. circular base and 1 vertex

B. 6 square faces

C. 2 triangular faces and 3 rectangular faces

D. 2 circular bases

E. 4 triangular faces

F. 6 rectangular faces

G. 1 square base and 4 triangular faces

Check What You Learned

Circles and Solid Figures

Answer each question. Use 3.14 for π.

14. In a circle, which is longer—the radius or the diameter?

The _____ is longer.

15. What is one of the formulas for finding the circumference of a circle?

One of the formulas is _____.

16. If the circumference of a circle is 42.39 cm, what is the diameter? What is the radius?

The diameter is _____ cm. The radius is _____ cm.

17. If the radius of a circle is 3 yards, what is the circle's circumference?

The circle's circumference is _____ yards.

18. What is the difference between a triangular pyramid and a square pyramid?

The difference is _____.

19. In a solid figure, what is an edge?

An edge is _____.

Check What You Know

Perimeter and Area

Find the perimeter of each figure.

a	b	c

1.

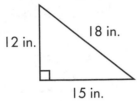

12 in.   18 in.   15 in.

$P =$ _____ in.

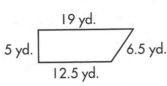

19 yd.   5 yd.   6.5 yd.   12.5 yd.

$P =$ _____ yd.

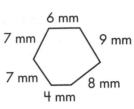

6 mm   7 mm   9 mm   7 mm   8 mm   4 mm

$P =$ _____ mm

Find the unknown measure, area, or perimeter.

2.

15 cm   11 cm

$A =$ _____ cm²

$P =$ _____ cm

$A = 247$ ft.² $W = 13$ ft.

$l =$ _____ ft.

$P =$ _____ ft.

$A = 81$ mm²

$s =$ _____ mm

$P =$ _____ mm

Find the area for the parallelogram or irregular shape.

3.

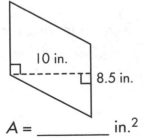

10 in.   8.5 in.

$A =$ _____ in.²

10 m   14 m   6 m   6 m

$A =$ _____ m²

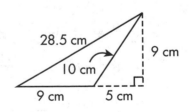

28.5 cm   9 cm   10 cm   9 cm   5 cm

$A =$ _____ cm²

NAME _____

Check What You Know

Perimeter and Area

Complete the chart for each circle. Use 3.14 for π. Round answers to the nearest hundredth.

	a Radius	**b** Diameter	**c** Area
4.	6 cm	_____ cm	_____ cm²
5.	_____ ft.	15 ft.	_____ ft.²
6.	_____ in.	_____ in.	78.5 in.²

Find the surface area of each solid figure.

a	**b**	**c**

7.

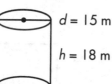

$d = 15$ m
$h = 18$ m

$A =$ _____ m²

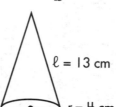

$\ell = 13$ cm
$r = 4$ cm

$A =$ _____ cm²

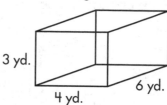

3 yd.
4 yd.
6 yd.

$A =$ _____ yd.²

8.

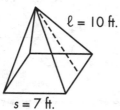

$\ell = 10$ ft.
$s = 7$ ft.

$A =$ _____ ft.²

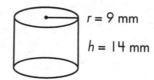

$r = 9$ mm
$h = 14$ mm

$A =$ _____ mm²

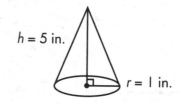

$h = 5$ in.
$r = 1$ in.

$A =$ _____ in.²

9. Elena needs to wrap a birthday present that is 23 cm long, 11.5 cm wide, and 6 cm high. What is the area of wrapping paper that she will need?

Elena will need _____ square centimeters of paper.

10. Keisha is making a round hook rug that is 3 yards in diameter. What is the area of the rug?

The rug is _____ square yards.

Lesson 8.1 Perimeter

The perimeter (P) is the distance around a figure. To find the perimeter, find the sum of the lengths of its sides. If two or more sides are equal, the formula can be simplified with multiplication.

Triangle	**Rectangle**	**Square**
$P = a + b + c$	$P = l + l + w + w$	$P = s + s + s + s$
	$P = 2l + 2w$	$P = 4s$

In the rectangle above, if the length is 6 cm and the width is 2 cm, the perimeter is:

$P = 2(6 \text{ cm}) + 2(2 \text{ cm}) = 12 \text{ cm} + 4 \text{ cm} = 16 \text{ cm}.$

Find the perimeter of each figure.

	a	**b**	**c**

1.

  1 ft. $\frac{3}{4}$ ft. $\frac{3}{4}$ ft.

10 yd. 10 yd. 10 yd. 20 yd.

1 in. $1\frac{3}{4}$ in. 2 in. $2\frac{1}{2}$ in.

_____ ft.   _____ yd.   _____ in.

2.

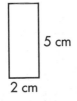 5 cm 2 cm

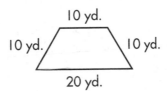 $2\frac{1}{3}$ ft. $5\frac{2}{3}$ ft.

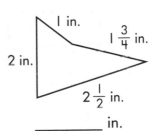 7 cm 4.6 cm 3.2 cm 4.4 cm

_____ cm   _____ ft.   _____ cm

3.

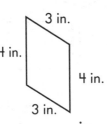 3 in. 4 in. 4 in. 3 in.

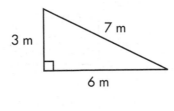 7 m 3 m 6 m

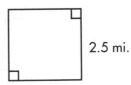 2.5 mi.

_____ in.   _____ m   _____ mi.

Lesson 8.2 Area of Rectangles

The **area (A)** of a figure is the number of square units inside that figure. Area is expressed in **square units** or **units²**.

The area of a square or rectangle is the product of its length and width.

$A = l \times w$

$A = 5 \text{ cm} \times 10 \text{ cm}$

$A = 50 \text{ cm}^2$

5 cm [rectangle] 10 cm

$A = s \times s$

$A = 5 \text{ cm} \times 5 \text{ cm}$

$A = 25 \text{ cm}^2$

5 cm [square]

If you know the area of a rectangle and either the length or width of a side, you can determine the unknown measurement.

$A = l \times w$

$24 \text{ m}^2 = 6 \text{ m} \times w$

$w = 24 \text{ m}^2 / 6 \text{ m}$

$w = 4 \text{ m}$

$A = 24 \text{ m}^2$

6 cm

Find the area of each rectangle below.

	a	**b**	**c**

1.
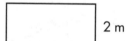 2 m
4 m

6 mi.

8 ft.
16 ft.

_____ m²   _____ mi.²   _____ ft.²

2.
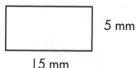 5 mm
15 mm

12 in.

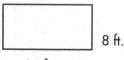 8 yd.
6 yd.

_____ mm²   _____ in.²   _____ yd.²

Find the unknown measure for each rectangle below.

3.
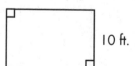 10 ft.

10.5 m

4 cm

$A = 150 \text{ ft.}^2$

$A = 23.1 \text{ m}^2$

$A = 44 \text{cm}^2$

$l = $ _____ ft.

$w = $ _____ m

$l = $ _____ cm

Lesson 8.3 Area of Parallelograms

A parallelogram is a polygon with two sets of parallel sides. To find the area of a parallelogram, multiply the measure of its base by the measure of its height: $A = b \times h$ or $A = bh$.

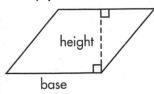

If $b = 8$ in. and $h = 7$ in., what is A?

$A = bh$

$A = 8$ in. $\times 7$ in. $= 56$ square inches or 56 in.^{2}

Find the area of each parallelogram.

| a | b | c |

1.

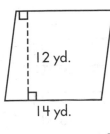

12 yd.

14 yd.

_____ yd.^{2}

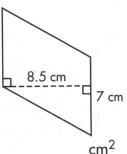

8.5 cm

7 cm

_____ cm^2

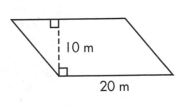

10 m

20 m

_____ m^2

2.

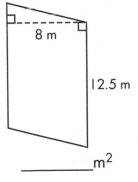

8 m

12.5 m

_____ m^2

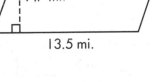

7.7 mi.

13.5 mi.

_____ mi.^{2}

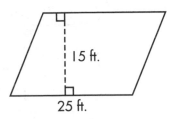

15 ft.

25 ft.

_____ ft.^{2}

3.

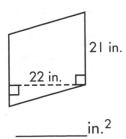

21 in.

22 in.

_____ in.^{2}

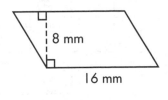

8 mm

16 mm

_____ mm^2

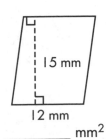

15 mm

12 mm

_____ mm^2

Lesson 8.4 Area of Irregular Shapes

To find the area of irregular shapes, separate the shapes into figures for which you can find the area.

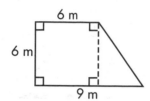

This figure can be divided into a square and a triangle.

Area of square:

$A = s \times s$

$A = 6 \text{ m} \times 6 \text{ m} = 36 \text{ m}^2$

Area of triangle:

$A = \frac{1}{2}bh$

$A = \frac{1}{2} \times 3 \text{ m} \times 6 \text{ m} = 9 \text{ m}^2$

The total area of the irregular shape = $36 \text{ m}^2 + 9 \text{ m}^2 = 45 \text{ m}^2$

Find the area of each figure.

a	b	c

1.

8 m, 12 m, 20 m, 16 m

$A = $ _____ m²

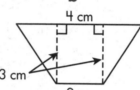
4 cm, 3 cm, 2 cm

$A = $ _____ cm²

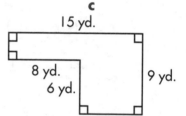
15 yd., 8 yd., 6 yd., 9 yd.

$A = $ _____ yd.²

2.

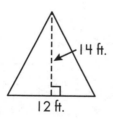
5 ft., 7 ft., 3 ft., 3 ft.

$A = $ _____ ft.²

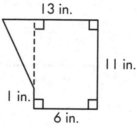
13 in., 11 in., 1 in., 6 in.

$A = $ _____ in.²

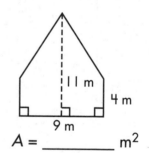
11 m, 4 m, 9 m

$A = $ _____ m²

3.

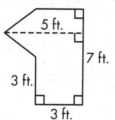
14 ft., 12 ft.

$A = $ _____ ft.²

3 mm, 6 mm, 3 mm, 3 mm, 3 mm, 3 mm, 6 mm

$A = $ _____ mm²

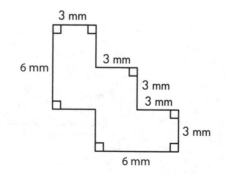
3 in., 4 in., 5.5 in.

$A = $ _____ in.²

Lesson 8.5 Area of a Circle

The area of a circle is the number of square units it contains. Like circumference, area is calculated using π, which represents about $3\frac{1}{7}$ or 3.14. The formula for finding the area of a circle is:

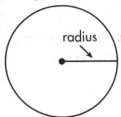

Area = π × radius × radius

$A = \pi r^2$

If a circle has a radius of 3 in., its area is π × 3 in. × 3 in. or about 28.6 in.^{2}
If a circle has a diameter of 7 in., its radius is $\frac{1}{2}$ of 7 in., or 3.5 in. In this example, the area = π × 3.5 in. × 3.5 in., or about 38.46 in.^{2}

Complete the chart for each circle described below. Use 3.14 for π. When necessary, round to the nearest hundredth.

	a Radius	b Diameter	c Area
1.	_____ mm	16 mm	_____ mm^2
2.	_____ ft.	12 ft.	_____ ft.^{2}
3.	4 yd.	_____ yd.	_____ yd.^{2}
4.	9 cm	_____ cm	_____ cm^2
5.	_____ mi.	5 mi.	_____ mi.^{2}
6.	_____ m	26 m	_____ m^2
7.	3.5 mm	_____ mm	_____ mm^2
8.	_____ in.	11.5 in.	_____ in.^{2}
9.	21 ft.	_____ ft.	_____ ft.^{2}
10.	_____ cm	30 cm	_____ cm^2

Lesson 8.6 Surface Area of a Pyramid

The **surface area (SA)** of a solid is the sum of the areas of all surfaces of the solid. The surface area of a square pyramid is the sum of the area of the square base and each of the four triangular sides.

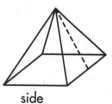

side

Each triangle's area is $\frac{1}{2}$ base × height. In a pyramid, base is the side length, and height is the slant height, or length. So surface area (SA) = area of square base + area of four triangular sides.

slant height, or length (ℓ) of the side

$SA = (\text{side} \times \text{side}) + 4(\frac{1}{2}\,\text{side} \times \text{length})$

$SA = s^2 + 2s\ell$

SA is given in square units, or units².

Find the surface area of each square pyramid.

| | a | b | c |

1.

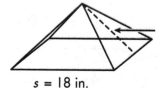

$\ell = 13.5$ in.
$s = 18$ in.

SA = _____ in.²

$\ell = 6$ yd.
$s = 8$ yd.

SA = _____ yd.²

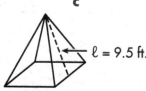

$\ell = 9.5$ ft.
$s = 7.5$ ft.

SA = _____ ft.²

2.

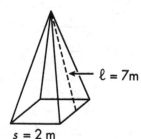

$\ell = 7$ m
$s = 2$ m

SA = _____ m²

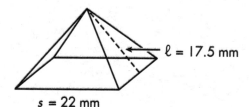

$\ell = 17.5$ mm
$s = 22$ mm

SA = _____ mm²

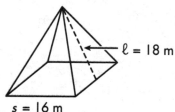

$\ell = 18$ m
$s = 16$ m

SA = _____ m²

3.

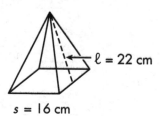

$\ell = 22$ cm
$s = 16$ cm

SA = _____ cm²

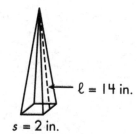

$\ell = 14$ in.
$s = 2$ in.

SA = _____ in.²

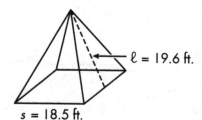

$\ell = 19.6$ ft.
$s = 18.5$ ft.

SA = _____ ft.²

Lesson 8.7 Surface Area of a Rectangular Solid

The surface area of a solid is the sum of the areas of all the faces (or surfaces) of the solid. A rectangular solid has six surfaces.

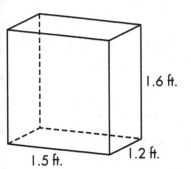

The area of each surface is determined by finding length × width, length × height, and width × height. Calculate the total surface area using the formula $SA = 2lw + 2lh + 2wh$.

In the figure on the left, $l = 1.5$ ft., $w = 1.2$ ft., and $h = 1.6$ ft.

$SA = 2(1.5 \text{ ft.})(1.2 \text{ ft.}) + 2(1.5 \text{ ft.})(1.6 \text{ ft.}) + 2(1.2 \text{ ft.})(1.6 \text{ ft.})$

$SA = 3.6 \text{ ft.}^2 + 4.8 \text{ ft.}^2 + 3.82 \text{ ft.}^2$

$SA = 12.22 \text{ ft.}^2$

1.6 ft.

1.5 ft.   1.2 ft.

Find the surface area of each figure.

| a | b | c |

1.

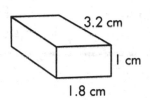

3.2 cm
1 cm
1.8 cm

$SA = $ _____ cm^2

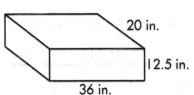

20 in.
12.5 in.
36 in.

$SA = $ _____ in.^{2}

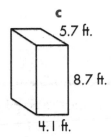

5.7 ft.
8.7 ft.
4.1 ft.

$SA = $ _____ ft.^{2}

2.

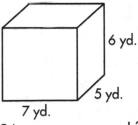

6 yd.
5 yd.
7 yd.

$SA = $ _____ yd.^{2}

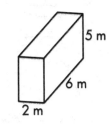

5 m
6 m
2 m

$SA = $ _____ m^2

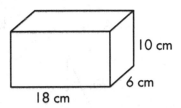

10 cm
6 cm
18 cm

$SA = $ _____ cm^2

3.

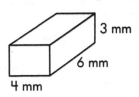

3 mm
6 mm
4 mm

$SA = $ _____ mm^2

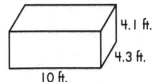

4.1 ft.
4.3 ft.
10 ft.

$SA = $ _____ ft.^{2}

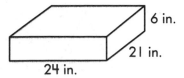

6 in.
21 in.
24 in.

$SA = $ _____ in.^{2}

Lesson 8.8   Surface Area of a Cone

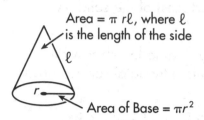

Area = $\pi\, r\ell$, where ℓ is the length of the side

ℓ

r

Area of Base = πr^2

The surface area (SA) of a cone is the sum of the area of the base plus the area of the top portion of the cone.

$$SA = \pi r\ell + \pi r^2 = \pi r(\ell + r)$$

If $\ell = 9$ in. and $r = 4$ in., what is the surface area of the cone? Use 3.14 for π.

$$SA = \pi r(\ell + r) = \pi 4 \text{ in.} (9 \text{ in.} + 4 \text{ in.}) = (3.14)52 \text{ in.}^2$$
$$= 163.28 \text{ in.}^2$$

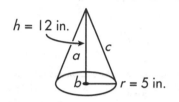

$h = 12$ in.

a c

b $r = 5$ in.

If you do not know the length of the side but do know the height of the cone, use the Pythagorean Theorem to find the length.

$$a^2 + b^2 = c^2$$
$$(12 \text{ in.})^2 + (5 \text{ in.})^2 = c^2$$
$$c^2 = 169 \text{ in.}^2$$
$$c = 13 \text{ in.} = \text{length } (\ell)$$

Therefore, $SA = \pi r(\ell + r) = \pi 5 \text{ in.} (13 \text{ in.} + 5 \text{ in.}) = (3.14)90 \text{ in.}^2$
$$= 282.6 \text{ in.}^2$$

Find the surface area of each figure.

a   **b**   **c**

1.

$\ell = 12$ ft.
$r = 8$ ft.

SA = _____ ft.^{2}

$\ell = 5$ cm
$r = 3$ cm

SA = _____ cm^2

$h = 20$ m
$r = 16$ m

SA = _____ m^2

2.

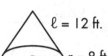

$h = 26$ mm
$r = 12$ mm

SA = _____ mm^2

$\ell = 22$ yd.
$r = 11$ yd.

SA = _____ yd.^{2}

$h = 8$ cm
$r = 8$ cm

SA = _____ cm^2

3.

$\ell = 10$ mm
$r = 5$ mm

SA = _____ mm^2

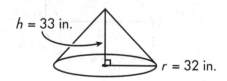

$h = 33$ in.
$r = 32$ in.

SA = _____ in.^{2}

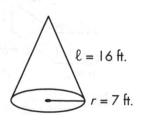

$\ell = 16$ ft.
$r = 7$ ft.

SA = _____ ft.^{2}

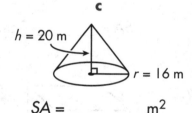
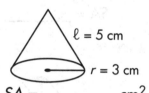

Lesson 8.9 Surface Area of a Cylinder

The surface area of a cylinder is the area of the circles plus the area of the round section in the middle. The surface area (SA) is found with the formula:

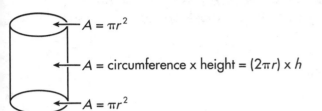

$A = \pi r^2$

$A = \text{circumference} \times \text{height} = (2\pi r) \times h$

$A = \pi r^2$

$SA = 2\pi r^2 + 2\pi rh$

In the figure on the left, if $r = 3$ cm and $h = 8$ cm, what is the surface area? Use 3.14 for π.

$SA = 2\pi r^2 + 2\pi rh$

$\quad = 2\pi (3 \text{ cm})^2 + 2\pi (3 \text{ cm})(8 \text{ cm})$

$\quad = 3.14(18 \text{cm}^2) + 3.14(48 \text{ cm}^2)$

$\quad = 207.24 \text{ cm}^2$

Find the surface area for each cylinder. Remember that $d = 2r$.

	a	b	c

1.

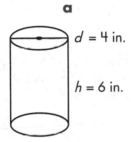

$d = 4$ in.

$h = 6$ in.

$SA = $ _____ in.^{2}

$d = 8$ mm

$h = 16$ mm

$SA = $ _____ mm^2

$d = 9$ ft.

$h = 9$ ft.

$SA = $ _____ ft.^{2}

2.

$r = 7$ cm

$h = 7$ cm

$SA = $ _____ cm^2

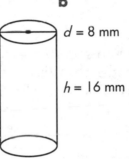

$d = 20$ in.

$h = 18$ in.

$SA = $ _____ in.^{2}

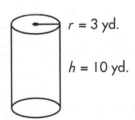

$r = 3$ yd.

$h = 10$ yd.

$SA = $ _____ yd.^{2}

3.

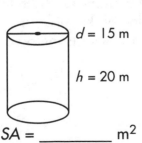

$d = 15$ m

$h = 20$ m

$SA = $ _____ m^2

$r = 13$ ft.

$h = 13$ ft.

$SA = $ _____ ft.^{2}

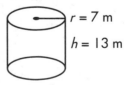

$r = 7$ m

$h = 13$ m

$SA = $ _____ m^2

NAME _____

Lesson 8.10 Problem Solving

Solve each problem. Use 3.14 for π. When necessary, round answers to the nearest hundredth.

1. Roberto's family is putting up a fence around their back yard. The yard is 75 feet long by 50 feet wide. How much fencing will Roberto's family need? How much space will Roberto have in which to play soccer?

   Roberto's family will need _____ feet of fencing.

   Roberto will have _____ square feet for soccer.

2. The students at Kennedy Middle School are painting a dunking booth for the school carnival. The booth measures 10 feet high, 8 feet wide, and 9 feet deep. How much surface area will they be painting?

   The students will be painting _____ square feet.

3. Tamara made a chocolate cake in a square baking pan. She can cut the cake into 20 pieces that measure 2 inches by 2 inches each. What is the total surface area of cake that she made? If the length of the pan is 10 inches, what is the width of the pan?

   The total surface area of the cake is _____ square inches.

   The width of the pan is _____ inches.

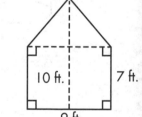

4. Trey drew a house for the school play, as shown on the right. The house is made up of a rectangle for the walls and a triangle for the roof. If Trey wants to paint the house, what area would he need to cover?

   The area of the house is _____ square feet.

5. Shannon is sewing a round table cloth for the kitchen table. The diameter of the table is 1.5 meters, and Shannon wants the tablecloth to hang over the edge of the table about 0.25 meter on each side. What is the total diameter of the tablecloth? What is the area of the tablecloth?

   The diameter of the tablecloth is _____ meters.

   The area of the tablecloth is _____ square meters.

NAME _____

Check What You Learned

Perimeter and Area

Find the perimeter of each figure.

a	b	c

1.

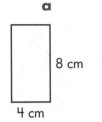

8 cm

4 cm

P = _____ cm

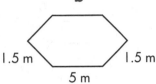

1.5 m   1.5 m

5 m

P = _____ m

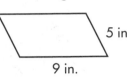

5 in.

9 in.

P = _____ in.

Find the unknown measure, area, or perimeter.

2.

A = 196 m²

s = _____ m

P = _____ m

5.5 yd.

7.5 yd.

A = _____ yd.²

P = _____ yd.

17 mm   41 mm

38 mm

A = _____ mm²

P = _____ mm

Find the area for the parallelograms and irregular shapes.

3.

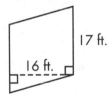

17 ft.

16 ft.

A = _____ ft.²

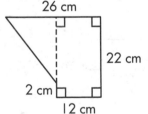

26 cm

22 cm

2 cm

12 cm

A = _____ cm²

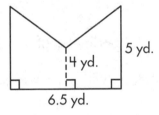

5 yd.

4 yd.

6.5 yd.

A = _____ yd.²

Complete the chart for each circle. Use 3.14 for π. Round answers to the nearest hundredth.

	a **Radius**	b **Diameter**	c **Area**
4.	3.5 yd.	_____ yd.	_____ yd.²
5.	_____ m	_____ m	201 m²

Check What You Learned

Perimeter and Area

Find the surface area of each solid figure.

a	b	c

6.

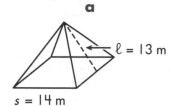

$\ell = 13$ m

$s = 14$ m

A = _____ m²

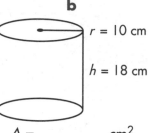

$r = 10$ cm

$h = 18$ cm

A = _____ cm²

$\ell = 12$ ft.

$r = 4$ ft.

A = _____ ft.²

7.

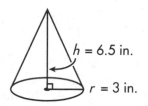

$h = 6.5$ in.

$r = 3$ in.

A = _____ in.²

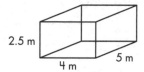

2.5 m

4 m   5 m

A = _____ m²

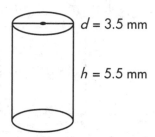

$d = 3.5$ mm

$h = 5.5$ mm

A = _____ mm²

8. Hope wants to walk three times around the mall. The mall measures 2,000 feet long by 1,000 feet wide. What is the perimeter of the mall? How many total feet will Hope walk?

The perimeter of the mall is _____ feet.

Hope will walk a total of _____ feet.

9. Caleb wants to paint a model rocket for his science project. The top part of the rocket is in the shape of a cone. It has a radius of 6 inches and a length of 12 inches. The bottom part of the rocket is in the shape of a cylinder. It has a diameter of 12 inches and a height of 18 inches. What is the total surface area that Caleb must paint?

The surface area of the cone is _____ square inches.

The surface area of the cylinder is _____ square inches.

Caleb must paint a total of _____ square inches.

Check What You Know

Volume

Find the volume of each figure.

1.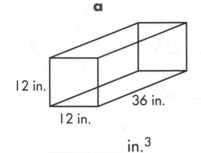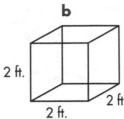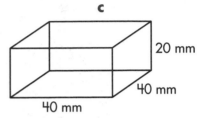

_____ in.³   _____ ft.³   _____ mm³

2.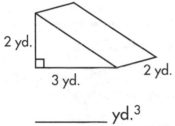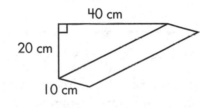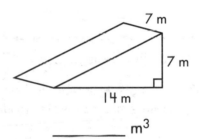

_____ yd.³   _____ cm³   _____ m³

3.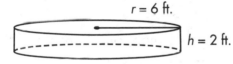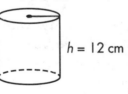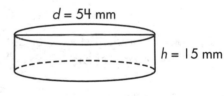

_____ ft.³   _____ cm³   _____ mm³

4.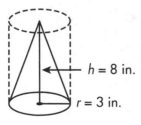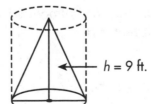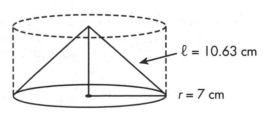

_____ in.³   _____ ft.³   _____ cm³

CHAPTER 9 PRETEST

Spectrum Geometry
Grades 6–8

Check What You Know
Chapter 9
91

Check What You Know

Volume

Find the volume of each figure.

a	b	c

5.

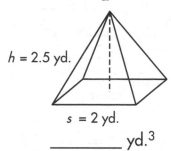

$h = 2.5$ yd.

$s = 2$ yd.

_____ yd.^{3}

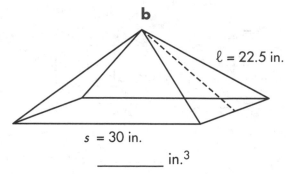

$\ell = 22.5$ in.

$s = 30$ in.

_____ in.^{3}

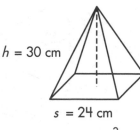

$h = 30$ cm

$s = 24$ cm

_____ cm^3

Solve each problem. Use 3.14 for π. Round answers to the nearest hundredth.

6. Jaime's water bottle has a diameter of 10 centimeters and a length of 30 centimeters. If Jaime fills the water bottle, how many cubic centimeters of water will it hold?

The water bottle's volume is _____ cubic centimeters.

7. Sonia bought a box of cat food that is 15 inches wide, 12 inches high, and 4 inches deep. How many cubic inches of cat food are in the box?

The box contains _____ cubic inches.

8. Antonio is filling paper cones with sugared almonds for the school fair. The paper cone is 7 inches deep and 3 inches in diameter at its widest. How many cubic inches of sugared almonds will each cone hold?

The cone will hold _____ cubic inches.

Lesson 9.1 Volume of Rectangular Prism

The **volume of a rectangular prism** is the product of the length times width times height. The product of the length times width is the base. The formula for the volume is $V = B \times h$. Because volume is measured in three dimensions, it is expressed in **cubic units,** or **units^3**.

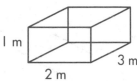

$B = 3 \times 2 = 6$

$V = B \times h = 6 \times 3.5$

$V = 21 \ m^3$

Find the volume of each rectangular prism.

	a	b	c

1.

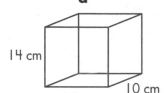

_____ cm^3

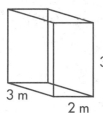

_____ m^3

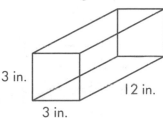

_____ in.^{3}

2.

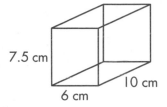

_____ cm^3

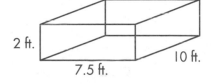

_____ ft.^{3}

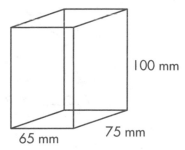

_____ mm^3

3.

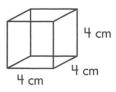

_____ cm^3

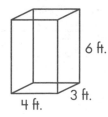

_____ ft.^{3}

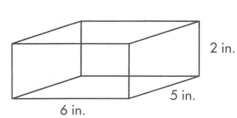

_____ in.^{3}

Lesson 9.2 Volume of Triangular Prisms

The **volume of a triangular prism** is the product of the area of the base (B) times the height. The base of a triangular prism is a triangle. To find the volume, multiply the area of one base times the height. Volume is expressed in **cubic units**, or **units³**.

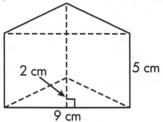

$B = \frac{1}{2}bh = \frac{1}{2}(9)(2) = 9$

$V = B \times h$

$V = 9 \times 5$

$V = 45 \text{ cm}^3$

Find the volume of each figure.

a	b	c

1.

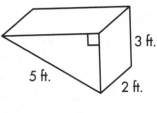

_____ ft.³

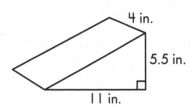

_____ in.³

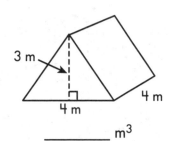

_____ m³

2.

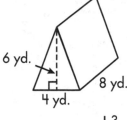

_____ yd.³

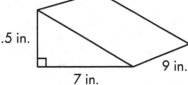

_____ in.³

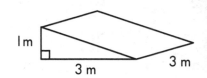

_____ m³

3.

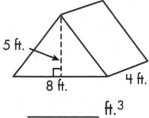

_____ ft.³

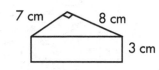

_____ cm³

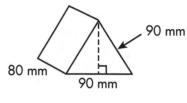

_____ mm³

Lesson 9.3 Volume of a Cylinder

The **volume of a cylinder** is the product of the area of the base *(B)* times the height. The formula for the volume of a cylinder is $V = B \times h$. Volume is expressed in **cubic units,** or **units³**.

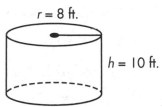

r = 8 ft.

h = 10 ft.

$V = B \times h$

$B = \pi r^2 = (3.14)(8)(8) = 200.96$

$V = 200.96 \times 10$

$V = 2009.6$ cubic feet

Find the volume of each figure. Round answers to the nearest hundredth. Remember, $d = 2r$.

	a	**b**	**c**

1.

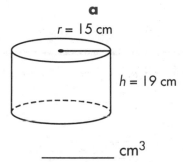
r = 15 cm
h = 19 cm
_____ cm³

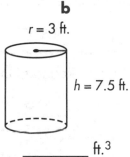
r = 3 ft.
h = 7.5 ft.
_____ ft.³

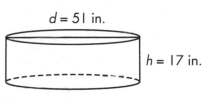
d = 51 in.
h = 17 in.
_____ in.³

2.

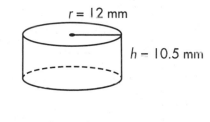
r = 12 mm
h = 10.5 mm
_____ mm³

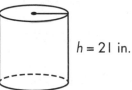
r = 10.5 in.
h = 21 in.
_____ in.³

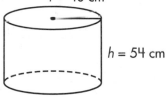
r = 40 cm
h = 54 cm
_____ cm³

3.

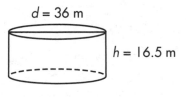
d = 36 m
h = 16.5 m
_____ m³

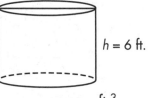
d = 8 ft.
h = 6 ft.
_____ ft.³

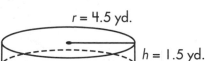
r = 4.5 yd.
h = 1.5 yd.
_____ yd.³

Lesson 9.4 Volume of a Cone

The **volume of a cone** is calculated as $\frac{1}{3}$ base × height. This is because a cone occupies $\frac{1}{3}$ of the volume of a cylinder of the same height.

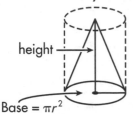

height →

Base = πr^2

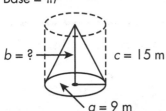

$b = ?$ $c = 15$ m

$a = 9$ m

Base is the area of the circle, πr^2. Volume is given in **cubic units**, or **units³**.

$$V = \frac{1}{3}\pi\, r^2 h$$

If the height of a cone is 7 cm and radius is 3 cm, what is the volume?

Use 3.14 for π. $V = \frac{1}{3}\pi\ 3^2 7$ $V = \pi\frac{63}{3}$ $V = \pi\ 21$ $V = 65.94$ cm³

If you do not know the height but you do know the radius and the length of the side, you can use the Pythagorean Theorem ($a^2 + b^2 = c^2$) to find the height. In this case, $b = 12$.

$$V = \frac{1}{3}\pi r^2 h = \frac{1}{3}\pi \times 81 \times 12 = 324\pi = 1017.36 \text{ m}^3$$

Find the volume of each cone. Use 3.14 for π. Round to the nearest hundredth. Remember that $d = 2r$.

	a	**b**	**c**

1.

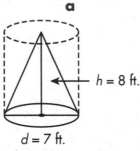

$h = 8$ ft.

$d = 7$ ft.

_____ ft.³

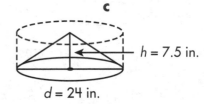

$h = 9$ m

$r = 10$ m

_____ m³

$h = 7.5$ in.

$d = 24$ in.

_____ in.³

2.

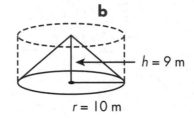

$h = 10$ cm

$r = 7.5$ cm

_____ cm³

$h = 7.5$ ft.

$d = 9$ ft.

_____ ft.³

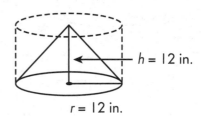

$h = 12$ in.

$r = 12$ in.

_____ in.³

3.

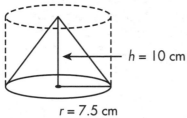

$\ell = 30$ ft.

$d = 36$ ft.

_____ ft.³

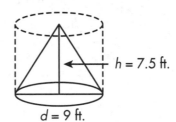

$h = 18$ ft.

$d = 21$ ft.

_____ cm³

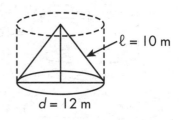

$\ell = 10$ m

$d = 12$ m

_____ m³

Lesson 9.5 Volume of a Pyramid

The **volume of a pyramid** is calculated as $\frac{1}{3}$ base × height. This is because a pyramid occupies $\frac{1}{3}$ of the volume of a rectangular prism of the same height.

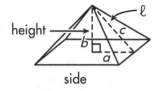

height ——

side

Because the base of a square pyramid is square, $B = s^2$.

So, $V = \frac{1}{3}Bh$ or $\frac{1}{3}s^2h$. Volume is given in **cubic units,** or **units³**.

If $s = 10$ cm and $h = 9$ cm, what is the volume?

$$V = \tfrac{1}{3}s^2h \quad V = \tfrac{1}{3}\,10^2 \times 9 \quad V = \tfrac{900}{3} \quad V = 300 \text{ cm}^3$$

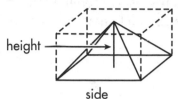

height ——

side

If you do not know the height but you do know the slant height or **length** of the side, you can use the Pythagorean Theorem to find the height.

$a = \frac{1}{2}$ of the side length, b = the height of the pyramid, c = length

If $s = 6$ m and $\ell = 5$ m, what is h? $a^2 + b^2 = c^2 \quad 3^2 + b^2 = 25 \text{ m} \quad b^2 = 16 \quad b = 4 \text{ m}$

Find the volume of each pyramid. Round answers to the nearest hundredth.

	a	**b**	**c**

1.

$h = 18$ cm

$s = 14$ cm

_____ cm³

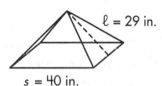

$\ell = 29$ in.

$s = 40$ in.

_____ in.³

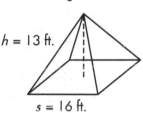

$h = 13$ ft.

$s = 16$ ft.

_____ ft.³

2.

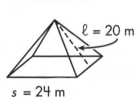

$\ell = 20$ m

$s = 24$ m

_____ m³

$\ell = 26$ mm

$s = 20$ mm

_____ mm³

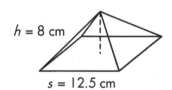

$h = 8$ cm

$s = 12.5$ cm

_____ cm³

3.

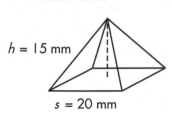

$h = 15$ mm

$s = 20$ mm

_____ mm³

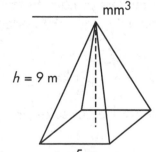

$h = 9$ m

$s = 5$ m

_____ m³

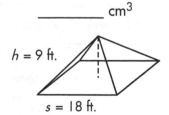

$h = 9$ ft.

$s = 18$ ft.

_____ ft.³

Lesson 9.6 Problem Solving

Solve each problem. Use 3.14 for π. Round answers to the nearest hundredth.

1. Aishani bought a chicken salad wrap in the shape of a cylinder, which was 15 centimeters long and had a radius of 7 centimeters. How many cubic centimeters of chicken salad did Aishani eat if she ate half of the wrap?

    Aishani ate _____ cm³.

2. Maddie is making melt-and-pour soap for her sister's birthday present. She is using a tray soap mold that makes four rectangular bars at a time. Each finished bar measures 2 inches wide, 3 inches long, and 1 inch deep. If Maddie makes one tray of soap, how much does she need to melt to fill the tray?

    Maddie needs to melt _____ in.³

3. Quon bought a wheel of brie cheese for his party. The cheese is 5 inches in diameter and $1\frac{1}{2}$ inches high. How many cubic inches of cheese are in the wheel Quon bought?

    The wheel of cheese contains _____ in.³

4. Marcus is making cupcakes for his daughter's birthday. His cupcake pan has recesses that are 6 centimeters in diameter and 4 centimeters deep. Marcus needs to fill each recess half-way. How many cubic centimeters of cake batter will each recess hold if Marcus fills it half-way? How many cubic centimeters of cake batter does Marcus need in order to make 12 cupcakes?

    The cake batter needed to make one cupcake is _____ cm³.

    The cake batter needed to make twelve cupcakes is _____ cm³.

Check What You Learned

Volume

Find the volume of each figure.

a	b	c

1.

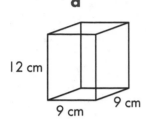

12 cm

9 cm 9 cm

_____ cm³

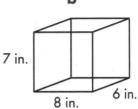

7 in.

8 in. 6 in.

_____ in.³

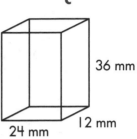

36 mm

24 mm 12 mm

_____ mm³

2.

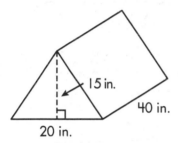

15 in.

20 in. 40 in.

_____ in.³

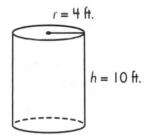

14 cm

24 cm

16 cm

_____ cm³

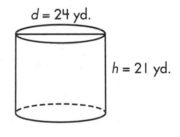

25 in.

60 in.

25 in.

_____ in.³

3.

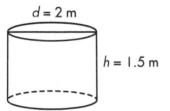

$d = 2$ m

$h = 1.5$ m

_____ m³

$r = 4$ ft.

$h = 10$ ft.

_____ ft.³

$d = 24$ yd.

$h = 21$ yd.

_____ yd.³

4.

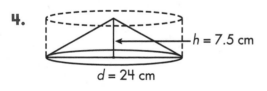

$h = 7.5$ cm

$d = 24$ cm

_____ cm³

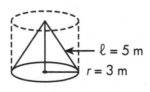

$\ell = 5$ m

$r = 3$ m

_____ m³

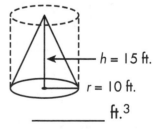

$h = 15$ ft.

$r = 10$ ft.

_____ ft.³

CHAPTER 9 POSTTEST

Spectrum Geometry
Grades 6–8

Check What You Learned
Chapter 9
99

Check What You Learned

Volume

Find the volume of each figure.

a	b	c

5.

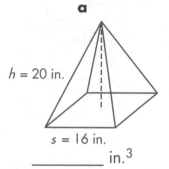

$h = 20$ in.

$s = 16$ in.

_____ in.^{3}

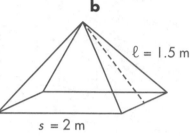

$\ell = 1.5$ m

$s = 2$ m

_____ m^3

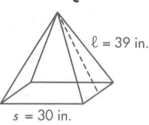

$\ell = 39$ in.

$s = 30$ in.

_____ in.^{3}

Solve each problem. Use 3.14 for π. Round answers to the nearest hundredth.

6. Ayesha is making salsa for her youth group's bake sale. She will be making enough salsa to fill 6 jars that are 3.2 inches in diameter and 5.5 inches tall. If she fills each jar with salsa up to 0.5 inch from the top of the jar, how many cubic inches does each jar contain? How many cubic inches of salsa will Ayesha prepare to make 6 jars of salsa?

One jar will contain _____ in.^{3}

Six jars will contain _____ in.^{3}

7. Han is making pyramid-shaped rice for the Math Club dinner. His rice mold makes square pyramids that are 7.5 centimeters on each side and 7 centimeters tall. How many cubic centimeters of rice will each pyramid contain? How many cubic centimeters of rice will Han need to prepare in order to serve 15 Math Club members?

One serving will contain _____ cm^3.

Fifteen servings will contain _____ cm^3.

8. Hope has filled a box with packing peanuts. If the box is 18 inches wide, 18 inches long, and 18 inches high, how many cubic inches of packing peanuts does Hope have?

The box contains _____ in.^{3}

Final Test Chapters 1–9

Use the figure to complete the following.

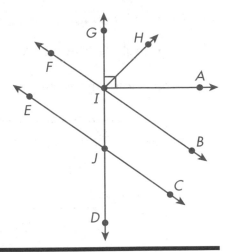

1. Name an angle that is vertical to ∠FIG._____

2. Is ∠EJD an acute angle, an obtuse angle, or a right angle? _____

3. Name an angle that is complementary to ∠HIA. _____

4. Name the transversal of $\overrightarrow{FB}$ and $\overrightarrow{EC}$. _____

5. What is a corresponding angle to ∠GIB. _____

Write a proportion for each problem. Then, solve the problem.

6. According to the map, a hiking trail is 12 centimeters long. If the map scale is 1 cm = 1.25 mi., how long is the trail?

   The trail is _____ miles long.

7. The petting zoo has three rabbits for every two goats. If there are 18 rabbits in the zoo, how many goats are there?

   The zoo has _____ goats.

Find the value of the variable in each equation.

	a	**b**	**c**
8.	$4 \times s = 16$ _____	$21 + 2b = 45$ _____	$p + 45 = 90$ _____
9.	$35t = 175$ _____	$\frac{410}{k} = 20$ _____	$6 \times 4a = 12$ _____

Final Test Chapters 1–9

Write an equation for the problem. Then, solve.

10. An angle is 65 degrees less than its supplement. Find the measure of each angle.

The angles measure _____ degrees and _____ degrees.

Find the lengths of the missing sides for the similar right triangles.

a	**b**	**c**

11.   AB = _____ in.   DE = _____ in.   DF = _____ in.

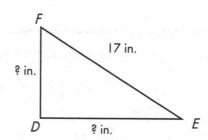

Use the figures to complete the statements and answer the questions.

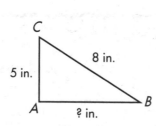

12. What is the sum of the measures of the interior angles in figure C? _____ °

Is figure C equiangular, equilateral, or regular? _____

13. Is figure D convex or concave? _____

14. What is figure A called? _____ What is figure B called? _____

What is the main difference between figure A and figure B? _____

15. In figure E, what is the sum of the measures of the interior angles? _____ °

What is the measure of each angle? _____ °

Final Test Chapters 1–9

Add or subtract the following integers.

	a	b	c
16.	7 + 11 = _____	2 − 1 = _____	7 − 18 = _____

Plot the following coordinates on the grid and connect the points by straight lines.

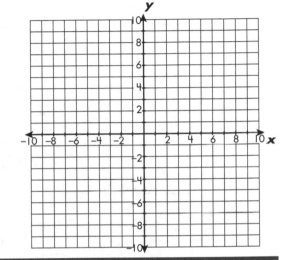

17. A(3, 3), B(6, 6), C(10, 6), D(7, 3)

E(3, −3), F(7, −3), G(10, −6), H(6, −6)

18. What type of polygon did you draw? _____

19. Is the transformation shown in the grid a translation, rotation, reflection, or dilation?

_____

Use the figure at the right to answer the questions.

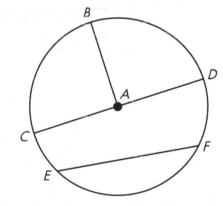

20. Name the circle. _____

21. Name the origin. _____

22. Name a radius. _____

23. Name a chord. _____

24. Name the diameter. _____

Complete the table below. Use 3.14 for π. If necessary, round answers to the nearest hundredth.

	a **Diameter**	b **Radius**	c **Circumference**	d **Area**
25.	_____ cm	_____ cm	31.4 cm	_____ cm
26.	42 in.	_____ in.	_____ in.	_____ in.
27.	_____ ft.	9 ft.	_____ ft.	_____ ft.

Final Test Chapters 1–9

Find the unknown measure of each shape.

a	**b**	**c**

28.

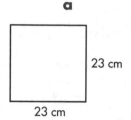

23 cm

23 cm

$P =$ _____

$A =$ _____

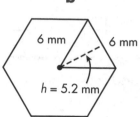

6 mm   6 mm

h = 5.2 mm

$P =$ _____

$A =$ _____

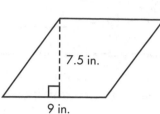

7.5 in.

9 in.

$P =$ _____

$A =$ _____

29.

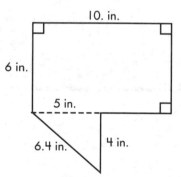

10. in.

6 in.

5 in.

6.4 in.   4 in.

$P =$ _____

$A =$ _____

6 mm

24 mm   8 mm

$SA =$ _____

$V =$ _____

6 cm   30 cm

18 cm

24 cm

$SA =$ _____

$V =$ _____

30.

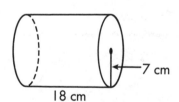

7 cm

18 cm

$SA =$ _____

$V =$ _____

h = 9 ft.   ℓ = 12.73 ft.

s = 18 ft.

$SA =$ _____

$V =$ _____

h = 9 ft.   ℓ = 10.3 ft.

r = 5 ft.

$SA =$ _____

$V =$ _____

Geometry Reference Chart

Formulas	
Perimeter of a rectangle (L8.1)	$P = 2l + 2w$
Area of a rectangle (L8.2)	$A = lw$
Perimeter of a square (L8.1)	$P = 4s$
Area of a square (L8.4)	$A = s \times s$
Perimeter of a triangle (L8.1)	$P = a + b + c$
Area of a triangle (L8.4)	$A = \frac{1}{2}bh$
Area of a circle (L8.5)	$A = \pi r^2$
Circumference of a circle (L7.2)	$C = 2\pi r \ (\pi = 3.14)$
Area of a parallelogram (L8.3)	$A = bh$
Surface area of a rectangular solid (L8.7)	$SA = 2lw + 2lh + 2wh$
Surface area of a cylinder (L8.9)	$SA = 2\pi r^2 + 2\pi rh$
Surface area of a cone (L8.8)	$SA = \pi r\ell + \pi r^2$
Surface area of a pyramid (L8.6)	$SA = s^2 + 2s\ell$
Volume of a rectangular prism (L9.1)	$V = lwh$
Volume of a triangular solid (L9.2)	$V = Bh$
Volume of a cylinder (L9.3)	$V = \pi r^2 h$
Volume of a cone (L9.4)	$V = \frac{1}{3}\pi r^2 h$
Volume of a pyramid (L9.5)	$V = \frac{1}{3}Bh$

Pythagorean Theorem

$$a^2 + b^2 = c^2$$

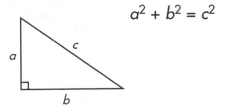

Triangles

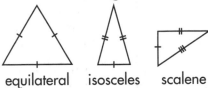

equilateral   isosceles   scalene

right angle   acute angle   obtuse angle

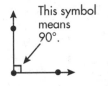
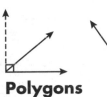
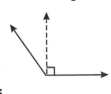

This symbol means 90°.

Polygons

Prefix	Name	Sides
tri-	triangle	3
quadri-	quadrilateral	4
penta-	pentagon	5
hexa-	hexagon	6
hepta-	heptagon	7
octa-	octagon	8
nona-	nonagon	9
deca-	decagon	10

Quadrilaterals

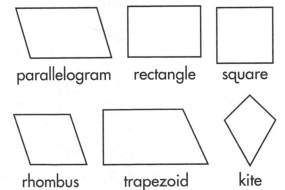

parallelogram   rectangle   square

rhombus   trapezoid   kite

Table of Squares and Square Roots

Except in the case of perfect squares, square roots shown on the chart are not exact.

Table of Squares and Square Roots					
n	n^2	$\sqrt{n}$	n	n^2	$\sqrt{n}$
1	1	1	51	2,601	7.14
2	4	1.41	52	2,704	7.21
3	9	1.73	53	2,809	7.28
4	16	2	54	2,916	7.35
5	25	2.24	55	3,025	7.42
6	36	2.45	56	3,136	7.48
7	49	2.65	57	3,249	7.55
8	64	2.83	58	3,364	7.62
9	81	3	59	3,481	7.68
10	100	3.16	60	3,600	7.75
11	121	3.32	61	3,721	7.81
12	144	3.46	62	3,844	7.87
13	169	3.61	63	3,969	7.94
14	196	3.74	64	4,096	8
15	225	3.87	65	4,225	8.06
16	256	4	66	4,356	8.12
17	289	4.12	67	4,489	8.19
18	324	4.24	68	4,624	8.25
19	361	4.36	69	4,761	8.31
20	400	4.47	70	4,900	8.37
21	441	4.58	71	5,041	8.43
22	484	4.69	72	5,184	8.49
23	529	4.80	73	5,329	8.54
24	576	4.90	74	5,476	8.60
25	625	5	75	5,625	8.66
26	676	5.10	76	5,776	8.72
27	729	5.20	77	5,929	8.77
28	784	5.29	78	6,084	8.83
29	841	5.39	79	6,241	8.89
30	900	5.48	80	6,400	8.94
31	961	5.57	81	6,561	9
32	1,024	5.66	82	6,724	9.06
33	1,089	5.74	83	6,889	9.11
34	1,156	5.83	84	7,056	9.17
35	1,225	5.92	85	7,225	9.22
36	1,296	6	86	7,396	9.27
37	1,369	6.08	87	7,569	9.33
38	1,444	6.16	88	7,744	9.38
39	1,521	6.24	89	7,921	9.43
40	1,600	6.32	90	8,100	9.49
41	1,681	6.40	91	8,281	9.54
42	1,764	6.48	92	8,464	9.59
43	1,849	6.56	93	8,649	9.64
44	1,936	6.63	94	8,836	9.70
45	2,025	6.71	95	9,025	9.75
46	2,116	6.78	96	9,216	9.80
47	2,209	6.86	97	9,409	9.85
48	2,304	6.93	98	9,604	9.90
49	2,401	7	99	9,801	9.95
50	2,500	7.07	100	10,000	10

Scoring Record for Posttests, Mid-Test, and Final Test

Chapter Posttest	Your Score	Performance			
		Excellent	Very Good	Fair	Needs Improvement
1	___ of 16	15–16	13–14	11–12	10 or fewer
2	___ of 14	13–14	12	11	10 or fewer
3	___ of 15	14–15	12–13	11	10 or fewer
4	___ of 11	11	10	9	8 or fewer
5	___ of 10	10	9	8	7 or fewer
6	___ of 17	15–17	13–14	11–12	10 or fewer
7	___ of 19	17–19	15–16	14	13 or fewer
8	___ of 9	9	8	7	6 or fewer
9	___ of 8	8	7	6	5 or fewer
Mid-Test	___ of 32	30–32	27–29	24–26	23 or fewer
Final Test	___ of 30	28–30	25–27	22–24	21 or fewer

Record your test score in the Your Score column. See where your score falls in the Performance columns. Your score is based on the total number of required responses. If your score is fair or needs improvement, review the chapter material.

Geometry Answers

Chapter 1

Check What You Know, page 1

	a	b	c
1.	line segment; $\overline{KJ}$, $\overline{JK}$, KJ	line; $\overleftrightarrow{FR}$, $\overleftrightarrow{RF}$, $\overleftrightarrow{FR}$	ray; $\overrightarrow{PQ}$, $\overrightarrow{PQ}$

2. ABC, FBG, DBE, GBF
3. ∠4, ∠5, ∠KLM
4. ∠NLM, ∠MLN

	a	b	c
5.	90°, right	130°, obtuse	80°, acute

Check What You Know, page 2

6. ∠CBH
7. ∠DBE
8. ∠EBA
9. 45°
10. ∠FBE
11. ∠7/∠3; ∠2/∠6
12. ∠1/∠5; ∠4/∠8
13. 25°
14. $\overleftrightarrow{QR}$
15. 60°
16. ∠4

Lesson 1.1, page 3

	a	b	c
1.	AB; BA	$\overrightarrow{AB}$; $\overrightarrow{BA}$	
2.	CD; DC	$\overleftrightarrow{CD}$; $\overleftrightarrow{DC}$	
3.	EF; FE	$\overleftrightarrow{EF}$; $\overleftrightarrow{FE}$	
4.	HG	$\overleftrightarrow{HG}$;	G; H
5.	KJ	$\overrightarrow{KJ}$;	J; K
6.			
7.			

Lesson 1.1, page 4

1. MKN; JKL
2. ABC; BDG, ADE
3. $\overleftrightarrow{LM}$; ML; $\overrightarrow{ML}$; LM
4. Any of the following: NO; $\overline{ON}$; $\overline{NO}$; ON

Lesson 1.2, page 5

	a	b
1.	CD, $\overrightarrow{CD}$	C
2.	EF, $\overrightarrow{EF}$	E
3.	GH, $\overrightarrow{GH}$	G

4. IJK, KJI, ∠IJK, ∠KJI, ∠J
5. LMN, NML, ∠LMN, ∠NML, ∠M

Lesson 1.2, page 6

1. ∠NLM, ∠MLN, ∠L, ∠4
   L, $\overrightarrow{LM}$ $\overrightarrow{LN}$
   $\overrightarrow{LM}$ $\overrightarrow{LN}$
2. ∠QOK, ∠KOQ, ∠O, ∠9
   O, $\overrightarrow{OK}$ $\overrightarrow{OQ}$
   $\overrightarrow{OK}$ $\overrightarrow{OQ}$
3. ∠6 or ∠CAD or ∠DAC; ∠7 or ∠DAE or ∠EAD;
   ∠CAE or ∠EAC
4. $\overrightarrow{AE}$, $\overrightarrow{AC}$

Lesson 1.3, page 7

	a	b
1.	120°; obtuse	60°; acute
2.	90°; right	30°; acute

Lesson 1.4, page 8

1. ∠IBD or ∠IBF
2. ∠GDF or ∠GDB or ∠GDA
3. ∠HDF
4. $\overrightarrow{DE}$
5. ∠MLO
6. ∠PLQ
7. 117°
8. 8°

Lesson 1.5, page 9

1. ∠1/∠2, ∠3/∠4, ∠5/∠6, ∠7/∠8
   ∠1/∠3, ∠2/∠4, ∠5/∠7, ∠6/∠8
2. ∠4/∠5
3. ∠2/∠7
4. ∠4/∠5, ∠6/∠7, ∠8/∠9, ∠10/∠11
   ∠5/∠7, ∠4/∠6, ∠9/∠11, ∠8/∠10
5. ∠9/∠6, ∠7/∠8
6. ∠11/∠4, ∠5/∠10

Geometry Answers

Lesson 1.6, page 10

1. 35°; 35°

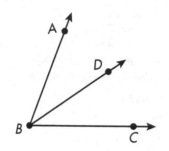

2. 70°; obtuse

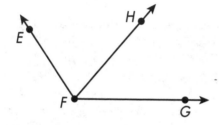

3. 60°; complementary

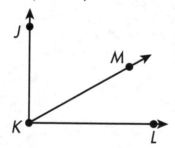

Check What You Learned, page 11

	a	b	c
1.	ray; $\overrightarrow{DE}$, DE	line segment; AB, BA, $\overline{BA}$	line; KM, MK, $\overleftrightarrow{MK}$

2. CBA, FBE, ABC, GBD
3. ∠7 or ∠QPR or ∠RPQ, ∠8 or ∠RPS or ∠SPR, ∠QPS
4. ∠RPS, ∠SPR

	a	b	c
5.	125°; obtuse	90°; right	50°; acute

Check What You Learned, page 12

6. ∠GJF
7. ∠ICD
8. ∠ACG or ∠BCJ or ∠DCI
9. 45°
10. ∠ECJ
11. ∠2/∠7; ∠3/∠6
12. ∠1/∠8; ∠4/∠5
13. 40°
14. $\overleftrightarrow{GH}$
15. 30°
16. 150°

Chapter 2

Check What You Know, page 13

	a	b	c
1.	12 = 12 ; T	35 ≠ 30	64 ≠ 25
2.	21 = 21 ; T	48 = 48 ; T	36 = 36 ; T
3.	105 = 105 ; T	20 ≠ 25	117 = 117 ; T
4.	20 ≠ 0	99 ≠ 33	42 = 42 ; T
5.	6	12	64
6.	22	1	3
7.	10	16	7.6
8.	8	2	2.2

Check What You Know, page 14

9. $\frac{1}{5} = \frac{n}{25}$; 5
10. $\frac{2}{3} = \frac{6}{n}$; 9
11. $\frac{1}{38} = \frac{n}{950}$; 25
12. $\frac{2}{3} = \frac{15}{n}$; 22.5
13. $\frac{6}{18} = \frac{1}{n}$; 3
14. $\frac{16}{7}$; 2.29

Lesson 2.1, page 15

	a	b	c
1.	6 = 6 ; T	50 ≠ 24	9 = 9 ; T
2.	16 ≠ 81	18 = 18 ; T	24 ≠ 25
3.	44 = 44 ; T	36 ≠ 21	126 = 126 ; T
4.	9 ≠ 12	60 = 60 ; T	36 ≠ 48
5.	360 = 360 ; T	72 = 72 ; T	26 = 26 ; T
6.	42 ≠ 36	35 ≠ 33	12 ≠ 48
7.	175 = 175 ; T	144 = 144 ; T	72 ≠ 84

Geometry Answers

Lesson 2.2, page 16

	a	b	c
1.	12	12	63
2.	20	9	60
3.	1	2.5	2

4. $\frac{1}{15} = \frac{5}{n}$; 75 oz.

5. $\frac{5}{1000} = \frac{n}{100,000}$; $500

Lesson 2.3, page 17

1. $\frac{1}{11} = \frac{20}{n}$; 220

2. $\frac{1}{5} = \frac{n}{305}$; 61

3. $\frac{6}{24} = \frac{1}{n}$; 4

4. $\frac{2}{5} = \frac{n}{70}$; 28

5. $\frac{27.5}{n} = \frac{1}{4}$; 110

Lesson 2.4, page 18

1. Answers will vary, depending on the dimensions students enter in the table. Make sure that they have calculated ratios in the table correctly. The answer to question 1 should be the ratio closest to 1.618.

2. $\frac{6}{n} = \frac{1.618}{1}$; 3.71 (rounded)

3. $6 + 3.71 = 9.71 \div 6 = 1.618$ (rounded)

Check What You Learned, page 19

	a	b	c
1.	$25 \neq 21$	$300 = 300$; T	$81 \neq 88$
2.	$65 \neq 64$	$112 = 112$; T	$85 = 85$; T
3.	$96 = 96$; T	$58 \neq 54$	$161 \neq 162$
4.	$90 = 90$; T	$246 = 246$; T	$72 \neq 88$
5.	32	8	3
6.	4	4.2	56
7.	45	30	40
8.	1	15	3

Check What You Learned, page 20

9. $\frac{5}{32} = \frac{1}{n}$; 6.4

10. $\frac{1}{4} = \frac{n}{0.8}$; 0.2

11. $\frac{15}{390} = \frac{1}{n}$; 26

12. $\frac{10}{15} = \frac{2}{n}$; 3

13. $\frac{5}{n} = \frac{0.5}{2}$; 20

14. $\frac{60}{n} = \frac{1.618}{1}$; 37.08

Chapter 3

Check What You Know, page 21

	a	b
1.	23; n	1; y
2.	$3 \times 5 > n$	$\frac{n}{3} + 2$ or $n \div 3 + 2$
3.	$\underline{4 \times 3}$; 2	$\underline{(5 - 2)}$; 36
4.	$\underline{6 \div 3}$; 11	$\underline{(2 + 5)}$; 10
5.	commutative	zero
6.	identity	associative
7.	$(6 \times 5) + (6 \times 4)$	$p \times (3 - 2)$
8.	$7 \times (d + e)$	$(5 \times r) - (5 \times 8)$

Check What You Know, page 22

	a	b	c
9.	16	243	216
10.	0.04	0.0156	0.1111
11.	30°	65°	45°
12.	70°	100°	52°
13.	21	11	6
14.	72	40	6
15.	$25.36 - n = 5.29$; $20.07		

Lesson 3.1, page 23

	a	b	c
1.	expression	equation	inequality
2.	inequality	expression	equation
3.	4; b	1; x	
4.	3; m	7; p	
5.	$7 + n = 8$	$n < 10$	
6.	$3 \times 6 > n$	$5n - 7$	

Lesson 3.2, page 24

	a	b
1.	$\underline{11 + 4}$; 12	$\underline{8 \times 9}$; 24
2.	$\underline{2 \times 3}$; 8	$\underline{15 \div 5}$; 1
3.	$\underline{6 \times 2}$; 15	$\underline{(3 + 7)}$; 100
4.	$\underline{66 \div 11}$; 1	$\underline{(11 - 3 - 2)}$; 11
5.	$\underline{4 \times 6}$; 22	$\underline{(10 + 4)}$; 42
6.	$\underline{18 \div 2}$; 30	$\underline{(2 + 7)}$; 6
7.	$\underline{(15 - 8)}$; 26	$\underline{(15 - 8)}$; 98

Lesson 3.3, page 25

	a	b
1.	commutative	identity
2.	associative	identity
3.	zero	commutative
4.	28	$5p \times n$
5.	0	$w + (9 + 7)$
6.	$(2f + g) + h$	$44y$
7.	0	$4fg \times (6g \times 9)$

Geometry Answers

Lesson 3.4, page 26

	a	b
1.	$(9 \times 3) - (9 \times 1)$	$(p \times q) + (p \times r)$
2.	$6 \times (7 + 8)$	$(15 \times 4) - (3 \times 4)$
3.	$7 \times (y + z)$	$(m \times 9) - (m \times 2) - (m \times p)$
4.	$(c \times h) + (d \times h)$	$r \times (r - y)$
5.	5	6
6.	1	3
7.	12	7

Lesson 3.5, page 27

	a	b	c
1.	4	11	0
2.	5	22	27
3.	101	63	17
4.	$14 + 8 + n = 38$; 16		
5.	$n + \$25.30 = \$52.27$; \$26.97		

Lesson 3.6, page 28

	a	b	c
1.	6	12	30
2.	12	52	15
3.	2	14	25
4.	$5 \times n = 20$ or $20 \div n = 5$ or $20 \div 5 = n$; 4		
5.	$605 = 55 \times n$ or $605 \div n = 55$ or $605 \div 55 = n$; 11		

Lesson 3.7, page 29

	a	b	c
1.	125	6,561	64
2.	144	243	83,521
3.	17,576	1,000	19,683
4.	6^5; 7,776	4^8; 65,536	5^2; 25
5.	8^3; 512	10^4; 10,000	3^4; 81
6.	7^5; 16,807	9^5; 59,049	12^3; 1,728

Lesson 3.8, page 30

	a	b	c
1.	$\frac{1}{4^3}$; 0.0156	$\frac{1}{6^2}$; 0.0278	$\frac{1}{5^4}$; 0.0016
2.	$\frac{1}{10^4}$; 0.0001	$\frac{1}{2^5}$; 0.0313	$\frac{1}{1^3}$; 1
3.	0.00137	0.00013	0.04
4.	0.0625	0.00024	0.00042
5.	0.00098	0.01235	0.00032
6.	0.00781	0.00412	0.00046

Lesson 3.9, page 32

	a	b	c
1.	15°	78°	57°
2.	47°	$90° - n°$	$90° - 4n°$
3.	55°	88°	35°
4.	67°	$180° - n°$	$180° - 5n°$
5.	60°	120°	60°
6.	$n + (n + 6) = 90$; 42; 48		
7.	$3n + n = 180$; 45; 135		

Check What You Learned, page 33

	a	b
1.	61; t	3; d
2.	$19 - n \times 5$	$15 - n < 7$
3.	$\underline{15 \div 5}$; 21	$\underline{8 \times 4}$; 38
4.	$\underline{(6 - 3)}$; 12	$\underline{(9 - 6)}$; 11
5.	0	$(6g + 4h) + k$
6.	$13m$	$11b + 2a$
7.	$(7 \times n) + (7 \times 6)$	$9 \times (f - p)$
8.	$h \times (11 + 5)$	$(m \times 6) + (m \times 7) + (m \times 8)$

Check What You Learned, page 34

	a	b	c
9.	1,296	3,125	512
10.	0.00137	0.00015	0.00292
11.	2°	77°	61°
12.	87	17	13
13.	150	19	8
14.	$\$1,000 \div n = \$125$ or $\$1,000 \div \$125 = n$; 8		
15.	$n + (n + 16) = 180$; 82; 98		

Chapter 4

Check What You Know, page 35

	a	b	c
1.	17°; obtuse	85°; acute	15°; 90°; right
2.	equilateral	isosceles	scalene
3.	$\frac{34}{51} = \frac{2}{3}$; $\frac{28}{42} = \frac{2}{3}$; $\frac{48}{72} = \frac{2}{3}$; similar		

	a	b
4.	25 m	34 ft.

Check What You Know, page 36

	a	b	c
5.	15	8	22
6.	8	9	8
7.	4	5	4
8.	$\sqrt{3,600}$; 60		
9.	$\sqrt{1,9296}$; 138.91		
10.	$\sqrt{8,955}$; 94.63		
11.	20 ft.		

	a	b	c
12.	40	144	108

Lesson 4.1, page 37

	a	b	c
1.	acute	obtuse	right
2.	40°; obtuse	40°; acute	90°, 35°; acute

Lesson 4.2, page 38

	a	b	c
1.	equilateral	scalene	isosceles
2.	equilateral	isosceles	equilateral

Geometry Answers

Lesson 4.3, page 39
1. $\frac{15}{30} = \frac{1}{2}$; $\frac{15}{30} = \frac{1}{2}$; $\frac{12}{24} = \frac{1}{2}$; similar
2. $\frac{25}{100} = \frac{1}{4}$; $\frac{60}{240} = \frac{1}{4}$; $\frac{80}{320} = \frac{1}{4}$; similar
3. $\frac{44}{88} = \frac{1}{2}$; $\frac{50}{100} = \frac{1}{2}$; $\frac{88}{168} = \frac{11}{21}$; not similar

Lesson 4.3, page 40

	a	b
1.	36 m	14 yd.
2.	384 in.	9 m
3.	175 cm	76 ft.

Lesson 4.4, page 41

	a	b	c
1.	3	9	7
2.	2	10	12
3.	15	14	18
4.	2	3	3
5.	8	9	9
6.	11	12	12
7.	9	10	9
8.	15	16	16

Lesson 4.5, page 42
1. $\sqrt{74} = 8.6$
2. $\sqrt{100} = 10$
3. $\sqrt{97} = 9.85$
4. $\sqrt{34} = 5.83$
5. $\sqrt{40} = 6.32$
6. $\sqrt{117} = 10.82$
7. $\sqrt{80} = 8.94$
8. $\sqrt{25} = 5$
9. $\sqrt{85} = 9.22$
10. $\sqrt{106} = 10.3$

Lesson 4.5, page 43
1. $\sqrt{36} = 6$
2. $\sqrt{112} = 10.58$
3. $\sqrt{160} = 12.65$
4. $\sqrt{132} = 11.49$
5. $\sqrt{48} = 6.93$
6. $\sqrt{2,200} = 46.9$
7. $\sqrt{820} = 28.64$

Lesson 4.6, page 44

	a	b	c
1.	80	15	25
2.	35	60	185
3.	225	480	1,020

Check What You Learned, page 45

	a	b	c
1.	20°; obtuse	50°; acute	90°, 25°; right
2.	scalene	isosceles	equilateral

3. $\frac{14}{84} = \frac{1}{6}$; $\frac{32}{192} = \frac{1}{6}$; $\frac{38}{228} = \frac{1}{6}$; similar

	a	b
4.	128 ft.	44 m

Check What You Learned, page 46

	a	b	c
5.	11	16	12
6.	9	10	9

7. $\sqrt{1213}$; 34.83
8. $\sqrt{6160}$; 78.49
9. $\sqrt{19968}$; 141.31
10. 39 ft.

	a	b	c
11.	270	120	150

Mid-Test (Chapters 1–4), page 47
1. ray
2. *ABE*, *GBC*
3. acute
4. ∠*CBE*
5. ∠*FBG*
6. 45°
7. ∠*ABG*, ∠*CBE*
8. ∠3, ∠6; ∠4, ∠5
9. ∠1, ∠8; ∠2, ∠7
10. 110°
11. $\overleftrightarrow{NO}$
12. ∠1 or ∠4

Mid-Test (Chapters 1–4), page 48

	a	b	c
13.	$6 \neq 48$	$22 = 22$; T	$24 = 24$; T
14.	$35 = 35$; T	$84 = 84$; T	$110 \neq 112$
15.	$\frac{2}{5} = \frac{10}{n}$; $n = 25$	$\frac{8}{n} = \frac{64}{3}$; $n = 0.38$	$\frac{8}{9} = \frac{n}{6}$; $n = 5.33$
16.	$\frac{7}{2} = \frac{n}{14}$; $n = 49$	$\frac{9}{3} = \frac{18}{n}$; $n = 6$	$\frac{2}{3} = \frac{n}{48}$; $n = 32$

17. $\frac{\$14}{\text{pie}} = \frac{\$700}{n \text{ pies}}$; $\$14n = \$700$; $n = 50$
18. $\frac{2 \text{ cm}}{1 \text{ ft.}} = \frac{l \text{ cm}}{14 \text{ ft.}}$; $l = 28$ cm; $\frac{2 \text{ cm}}{1 \text{ ft.}} = \frac{w \text{ cm}}{12 \text{ ft.}}$; $w = 24$ cm
19. $1.618 = \frac{l}{530 \text{ m}}$; $l = 1.618(530 \text{ m}) = 857.5$ m

Geometry Answers

Mid-Test (Chapters 1–4), page 49

20. $2s + r$; $12w$
21. $(6g + 4h) + k$; $10p - 5p$
22. $4(x + z)$; 0

	a	**b**	**c**
23.	$a = 16$	$b = 18$	$n = 3$
24.	$\frac{1}{9} = 0.11$	$5^3 = 125$	$\frac{4^4}{2^3} = \frac{256}{8} = 32$
25.	$45°$	$135°$	$180° - s°$

26. $n + (n + 25) = 90$; $32.5°$; $57.5°$

Mid-Test (Chapters 1–4), page 50

27. $\frac{18}{25} = 0.72$ in.; $\frac{10}{12} = 0.83$ in.; $\frac{15}{22} = 0.68$ in.; not similar
28. $\sqrt{56} = 7.5$
29. $\sqrt{100} = 10$
30. $\sqrt{23,775} = 154.2$
31. $mast^2 = 12^2 - 7^2$; $mast^2 = 144 - 49$; $mast = \sqrt{95}$, or 9.75 ft.

	a	**b**	**c**
32.	30 cm	10 cm	8 cm

Chapter 5

Check What You Know, page 51

1a. decagon; 1440°; 144°
1b. quadrilateral; 360°; 90°
1c. hexagon; 720°; 120°
2a. heptagon; 900°; 128.57°
2b. octagon; 1080°; 135°
2c. pentagon; 540°; 108°
3a. quadrilateral; equilateral
3b. triangle; regular
3c. hexagon; equiangular

Check What You Know, page 52

4. parallelogram; opposite
5. parallel; kite
6. rectangle; parallelogram
7. square; congruent
8. A, C; A, D; B, D; B, E; C, E
9. concave

	a	**b**
10.	$\frac{AB}{EF} = \frac{BD}{FH}$	$\frac{KL}{NO} = \frac{LM}{OP}$
	$\frac{28}{42} = \frac{22}{33}$ similar	$\frac{14}{42} \neq \frac{18}{72}$ not similar

Lesson 5.1, page 53

1a. decagon; 1440°; 144°
1b. hexagon; 720°; 120°
1c. triangle; 180°; 60°
2a. quadrilateral; equilateral
2b. heptagon; regular
2c. quadrilateral; equiangular

Lesson 5.1, page 54

1a. A, C; A, D; B, D; B, E; C, E; convex

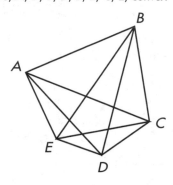

1b. F, H; F, I; G, I; G, J; H, J; concave

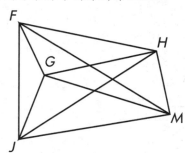

2a. K, M; L, N; convex

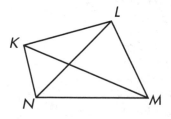

2b. W, Y; X, Z; convex

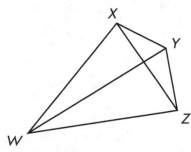

Geometry Answers

Lesson 5.2, page 55

1. square, rectangle, rhombus
2. rectangle, parallelogram
3. D has 4 congruent sides.
4. trapezoid
5. 65°
6. rhombus, parallelogram
7. 70°
8. kite

Lesson 5.3, page 56

	a	b
1.	$\frac{AB}{EF} = \frac{BD}{FH}$	$\frac{IK}{MO} = \frac{IJ}{MN}, \frac{JL}{NP} = \frac{LK}{PO}$
	$\frac{84}{12} = \frac{56}{8}$ similar	$\frac{30}{12} = \frac{20}{8}, \frac{25}{10} = \frac{10}{4}$ similar
2.	$\frac{QR}{TU} = \frac{QS}{TV}$	$\frac{AC}{WY} = \frac{CD}{YZ}, \frac{DB}{ZX} = \frac{AB}{WX}$
	$\frac{9}{16} \neq \frac{8}{16}$ not similar	$\frac{22}{88} = \frac{18}{72}, \frac{32}{128} = \frac{12}{48}$ similar

Check What You Learned, page 57

1a. pentagon; 540°; 108°
1b. octagon; 1080°; 135°
1c. triangle; 180°; 60°
2a. quadrilateral; 360°; 90°
2b. nonagon; 1260°; 140°
2c. heptagon; 900°; 128.57°
3a. pentagon; equiangular
3b. hexagon; regular
3c. quadrilateral; equilateral

Check What You Learned, page 58

4. trapezoid; bases; legs
5. 360°; 70°
6. parallelogram; 128°
7. 90°
8. Figure D: A, C; B, D; Figure E: J, L; J, M; K, M; K, N; L, N
9. Figure E

	a	b
10.	$\frac{AB}{EF} = \frac{BD}{FH}, \frac{AC}{EG} = \frac{CD}{GH}$	$\frac{JK}{NO} = \frac{KM}{OQ}$
	$\frac{18}{12} = \frac{30}{20}$ similar	$\frac{30}{10} \neq \frac{20}{8}$ not similar

Chapter 6

Check What You Know, page 59

	a	b	c
1.	−16	0	−21
2.	6	5	−11
3.	14	−20	9
4.	7	−5	0

5. E, G
6. D, B
7. (2, 6), (6, 5)
8. (2, 2), (4, 7)

9.–11.

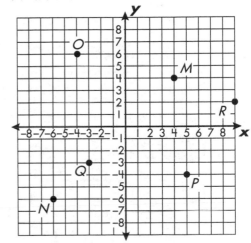

Check What You Know, page 60

12. reflection
13. A(−5, 3), B(−4, 4), C(−3, 3), D(−4, 2)
14. A'(−6, −4), B'(−4, −2), C'(−2, −4), D'(−4, −6)
15. dilation
16.

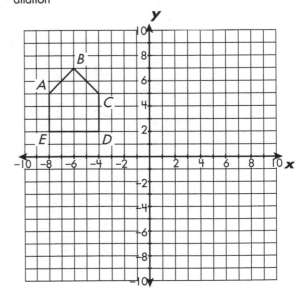

17. pentagon

Geometry Answers

Lesson 6.1, page 61

	a	b	c
1.	9	8	8
2.	−7	−9	12
3.	−35	−9	−20
4.	−12	−22	−11
5.	0	2	1
6.	−10	11	−19

Lesson 6.2, page 62

1. H, E
2. D, G
3. L(9, 5), C(3, 3)
4. J(1, 8), I(5, 3)
5. F(8, 8), K(7, 4)

6.–7.

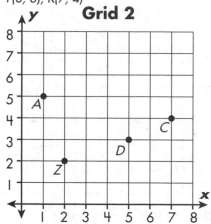

Grid 2

Lesson 6.2, page 63

1.–5.

Grid 1

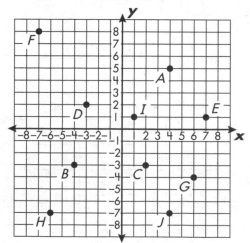

6. A(7, 6), B(−2, 5)
7. C(−3, −2), D(3, −3)
8. E(−4, 7), F(−4, −6)
9. G(5, 4), H(7, −4)
10. I(−8, −5), J(−6, 2)

Lesson 6.3, page 64

1a. dilation
1b. rotation
1c. translation or reflection
2a. rotation
2b. reflection
2c. dilation
3a. reflection
3b. translation or reflection
3c. translation

Lesson 6.3, page 65

1. A(1, −4), B(4, −1), C(7, −4)
2. A′(1, 4), B′(4, 1), C′(7, 4)
3. reflection
4. A(3, −1), B(5, −2), C(3, −4), D(1, −3)
5.

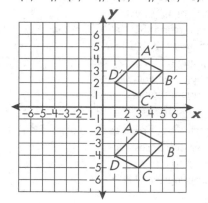

6. translation

Geometry Answers

Lesson 6.4, page 66

1. trapezoid

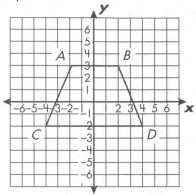

2. quadrilateral

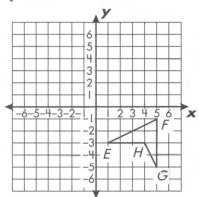

3. parallelogram

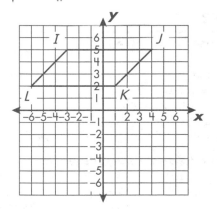

Check What You Learned, page 67

	a	b	c
1.	14	–3	–26
2.	–6	–4	–11
3.	15	17	–9
4.	–4	41	2

5. B, E
6. C, G
7. A(10, 5), H(7, 4)
8. F(4, 9), D(1, 1)

9.–11. **Grid 1**

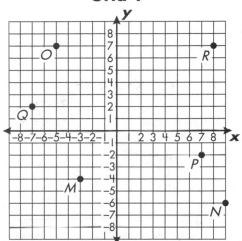

Check What You Learned, page 68

12. rotation
13. A(1, –3), B(3, –1), C(6, –1), D(4, –3)
14. A'(–6, 2), B'(–4, 4), C'(–1, 4), D'(–3, 2)
15. translation
16.

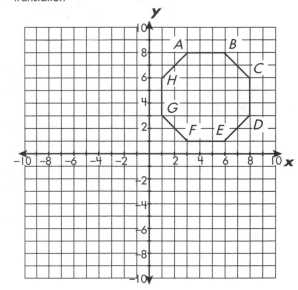

17. octagon

Geometry Answers

Chapter 7

Check What You Know, page 69

1. C
2. C
3. $\overline{CD}$, $\overline{CE}$, $\overline{CF}$
4. $\overline{EF}$, $\overline{GH}$
5. $\overline{EF}$
6. 87.92 in.; 75.36 cm; 106.76 yd.
7. E
8. G
9. B
10. F
11. C
12. D
13. A

Check What You Know, page 70

14. radius
15. origin
16. 5 ft.; 2.5 ft.
17. 37.68 ft.
18. cylinder
19. square

Lesson 7.1, page 71

	a	b	c
1.	radius	diameter	chord

2. A   **3.** A
4. $\overline{AB}$, $\overline{AC}$, $\overline{AD}$ **5.** $\overline{CD}$, $\overline{EF}$ **6.** $\overline{CD}$
7. Answers will vary. One possible answer is shown.

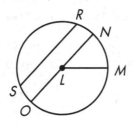

Lesson 7.2, page 72

	a	b	c
1.	3 ft.	1.5 ft.	9.42 ft.
2.	37 cm	18.5 cm	116.18 cm
3.	24 yd.	12 yd.	75.36 yd.
4.	4.5 mm	2.25 mm	14.13 mm
5.	10 km	5 km	31.4 km
6.	24.2 in.	12.1 in.	75.99 in.
7.	10.5 mi.	5.25 mi.	32.97 mi.
8.	1.5 cm	0.75 cm	4.71 cm
9.	9.6 ft.	4.8 ft.	30.14 ft.

Lesson 7.3, page 73

1. triangular pyramid
2. rectangular solid
3. cylinder
4. triangular solid
5. square pyramid
6. cone
7. 4 faces; triangular
8. 6 faces; rectangular
9. 2 faces; circular
10. 5 faces; 2 triangular, 3 rectangular
11. 5 faces; 1 square, 4 triangular
12. 1 face; circular

Lesson 7.4, page 74

1. Shaylin   **2.** diameter   **3.** 6 in.; 3 in.
4. 6.28 ft.   **5.** cube   **6.** cylinder

Check What You Learned, page 75

1. origin   **2.** diameter   **3.** radius
4. chord   **5.** A
6. 6 mi.; 226.08 ft.; 18 mm
7. D **8.** E **9.** G **10.** A **11.** F **12.** C **13.** B

Check What You Learned, page 76

14. diameter
15. $C = \pi \times d$ or $C = 2 \times \pi \times r$
16. 13.5 cm; 6.75 cm
17. 18.84 yd.
18. The square pyramid has 1 square base.
19. the intersection of 2 faces

Chapter 8

Check What You Know, page 77

	a	b	c
1.	45 in.	43 yd.	41 mm
2a.	$A = 165$ cm^2; $P = 52$ cm		
2b.	$l = 19$ ft.; $P = 64$ ft.		
2c.	$s = 9$ mm; $P = 36$ mm		
3.	85 in.^{2}	100 m^2	40.5 cm^2

Check What You Know, page 78

	a	b	c
4.	6 cm	12 cm	113.04 cm^2
5.	7.5 ft.	15 ft.	176.63 ft.^{2}
6.	5 in.	10 in.	78.5 in.^{2}
7.	1201.05 m^2	213.52 cm^2	108 yd.^{2}
8.	189 ft.^{2}	1299.96 mm^2	19.15 in.^{2}
9.	943 cm^2		
10.	7.07 yd.^{2}		

Geometry Answers

Lesson 8.1, page 79

	a	b	c
1.	$2\frac{1}{2}$ ft.	50 yd.	$7\frac{1}{4}$ in.
2.	14 cm	16 ft.	19.2 cm
3.	14 in.	16 m	10 mi.

Lesson 8.2, page 80

	a	b	c
1.	8 m^2	36 mi.^{2}	12.8 ft.^{2}
2.	75 mm^2	144 in.^{2}	48 yd.^{2}
3.	15 ft.	2.2 m	11 cm

Lesson 8.3, page 81

	a	b	c
1.	168 yd.^{2}	59.5 cm^2	200 m^2
2.	100 m^2	103.95 mi.^{2}	375 ft.^{2}
3.	462 in.^{2}	128 mm^2	180 mm^2

Lesson 8.4, page 82

	a	b	c
1.	288 m^2	9 cm^2	87 yd.^{2}
2.	25 ft.^{2}	101 in.^{2}	67.5 m^2
3.	84 ft.^{2}	45 mm^2	19.25 in.^{3}

Lesson 8.5, page 83

	a	b	c
1.	8 mm	16 mm	200.96 mm^2
2.	6 ft.	12 ft.	113.04 ft.^{2}
3.	4 yd.	8 yd.	50.24 yd.^{2}
4.	9 cm	18 cm	254.34 cm^2
5.	2.5 mi.	5 mi.	19.63 mi.^{2}
6.	13 m	26 m	530.66 m^2
7.	3.5 mm	7 mm	38.47 mm^2
8.	5.75 in.	11.5 in.	103.82 in.^{2}
9.	21 ft.	42 ft.	1,384.74 ft.^{2}
10.	15 cm	30 cm	706.5 cm^2

Lesson 8.6, page 84

	a	b	c
1.	810 in.^{2}	160 yd.^{2}	198.75 ft.^{2}
2.	32 m^2	1,254 mm^2	832 m^2
3.	960 cm^2	60 in.^{2}	1,067.45 ft.^{2}

Lesson 8.7, page 85

	a	b	c
1.	21.52 cm^2	2,840 in.^{2}	217.26 ft.^{2}
2.	214 yd.^{2}	104 m^2	696 cm^2
3.	108 mm^2	203.26 ft.^{2}	1,548 in.^{2}

Lesson 8.8, page 86

	a	b	c
1.	502.4 ft.^{2}	75.36 cm^2	2,090.49 m^2
2.	1,531.32 mm^2	1,139.82 yd.^{2}	485.07 cm^2
3.	235.5 mm^2	7,834.43 in.^{2}	505.54 ft.^{2}

Lesson 8.9, page 87

	a	b	c
1.	100.48 in.^{2}	502.4 mm^2	381.51 ft.^{2}
2.	615.44 cm^2	1758.4 in.^{2}	244.92 yd.^{2}
3.	1,295.25 m^2	2,122.64 ft.^{2}	879.2 m^2

Lesson 8.10, page 88

1.	250 ft.; 3750 ft.^{2}
2.	484 ft.^{2}
3.	80 in.^{2}; 8 in.
4.	76.5 ft.^{2}
5.	2 m; 3.14 m^2

Check What You Learned, page 89

	a	b	c
1.	24 cm	16 m	28 in.
2a.	$s = 14$ m; $P = 56$ m		
2b.	$A = 41.25$ yd.^{2}; $P = 26$ yd.		
2c.	$A = 323$ mm^2; $P = 96$ mm		
3.	272 ft.^{2}	404 cm^2	29.25 yd.^{2}
4.	3.5 yd.	7 yd.	38.47 yd.^{2}
5.	8 m	16 m	201 m^2

Check What You Learned, page 90

	a	b	c
6.	560 m^2	1,758.4 cm^2	200.96 ft.^{2}
7.	95.71 in.^{2}	85 m^2	79.68 mm^2
8.	6,000 ft.; 18,000 ft.		
9.	339.12 in.^{2}; 904.32 in.^{2}; 1,243.44 in.^{2}		

Chapter 9

Check What You Know, page 91

	a	b	c
1.	5,184 in.^{3}	8 ft.^{3}	32,000 mm^3
2.	6 yd.^{3}	4,000 cm^3	343 m^3
3.	226.08 ft.^{3}	1,356.48 cm^3	34,335.9 mm^3
4.	75.36 in.^{3}	150.72 ft.^{3}	410.29 cm^3

Check What You Know, page 92

	a	b	c
5.	3.33 yd.^{3}	5,031 in.^{3}	5,760 cm^3
6.	2,355 cm^3		
7.	720 in.^{3}		
8.	16.49 in.^{3}		

Lesson 9.1, page 93

	a	b	c
1.	2,240 cm^3	6 m^3	108 in.^{3}
2.	450 cm^3	150 ft.^{3}	487,500 mm^3
3.	64 cm^3	72 ft.^{3}	60 in.^{3}

Geometry Answers

Lesson 9.2, page 94

	a	b	c
1.	15 ft.^{3}	121 in.^{3}	24 m^3
2.	96 yd.^{3}	110.25 in.^{3}	4.5 m^3
3.	80 ft.^{3}	84 cm^3	324,000 mm^3

Lesson 9.3, page 95

	a	b	c
1.	13,423.5 cm^3	211.95 ft.^{3}	34,710.35 in.^{3}
2.	4,747.68 mm^3	7,269.89 in.^{3}	271,296 cm^3
3.	16,786.44 m^3	301.44 ft.^{3}	95.38 yd.^{3}

Lesson 9.4, page 96

	a	b	c
1.	102.57 ft.^{3}	942 m^3	1,130.4 in.^{3}
2.	588.75 cm^3	158.96 ft.^{3}	1,808.64 in.^{3}
3.	8,138.88 ft.^{3}	2,077.11 cm^3	301.44 m^3

Lesson 9.5, page 97

	a	b	c
1.	1,176 cm^3	11,200 in.^{3}	1,109.33 ft.^{3}
2.	3,072 m^3	3,200 mm^3	416.67 cm^3
3.	2,000 mm^3	75 m^3	972 ft.^{3}

Lesson 9.6, page 98

1. 1,153.95 cm^3
2. 24 in.^{3}
3. 29.44 in.^{3}
4. 56.52 cm^3 for each cupcake; 678.24 cm^3 for 12 cupcakes

Check What You Learned, page 99

	a	b	c
1.	972 cm^3	336 in.^{3}	10,368 mm^3
2.	6,000 in.^{3}	2,688 cm^3	18,750 in.^{3}
3.	4.71 m^3	502.4 ft.^{3}	9,495.36 yd.^{3}
4.	1,130.4 cm^3	37.68 m^3	1,570 ft.^{3}

Check What You Learned, page 100

5. 1,706.67 in.^{3} 1.49 m^3 10,800 in.^{3}
6. 40.19 in.^{3} for one jar; 241.15 in.^{3} for six jars
7. 131.25 cm^3 for one serving; 1,968.75 cm^3 for fifteen servings
8. 5,832 in.^{3}

Final Test, Page 101

1. $\angle JIB$
2. obtuse
3. $\angle HIG$
4. $\overleftrightarrow{GD}$
5. $\angle IJC$
6. $\frac{1 \text{ cm}}{1.25 \text{ mi.}} = \frac{12 \text{ cm}}{x \text{ mi.}}$; $x = 15$ miles
7. $\frac{3 \text{ rabbits}}{2 \text{ goats}} = \frac{18 \text{ rabbits}}{y \text{ goats}}$; $y = 12$ goats

	a	b	c
8.	$s = 4$	$b = 12$	$p = 45$
9.	$t = 5$	$k = 20.5$	$a = 0.5$

Final Test, Page 102

10. $n = (180 - n) - 65$; 57.5 degrees; 122.5 degrees

	a	b	c
11.	6.2 in.	13.2 in.	10.6 in.

12. 360°; equiangular
13. convex
14. trapezoid; rhombus; A trapezoid has only one pair of parallel sides while a rhombus has two.
15. 720°; 120°

Geometry Answers

Final Test, Page 103

	a	b	c
16.	18	1	−11

17.

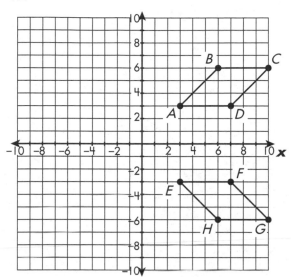

18. rhombus
19. reflection
20. A
21. A
22. $\overline{AB}$, $\overline{AD}$, $\overline{AC}$
23. $\overline{CD}$, $\overline{EF}$
24. $\overline{CD}$

	a	b	c	d
25.	10	5	31.4	78.5
26.	42	21	131.88	1,384.74
27.	18	9	56.52	254.34

Final Test, Page 104

	a	b	c
28.	$P = 92$ cm $A = 529$ cm^2	$P = 36$ mm $A = 93.6$ mm^2	$P = 36$ in. $A = 67.5$ in.^{2}
29.	$P = 37.4$ in. $A = 70$ in.^{2}	$SA = 768$ mm^2 $V = 1,152$ mm^3	$SA = 864$ cm^2 $V = 1,296$ cm^3
30.	$SA = 1,099$ cm^2 $V = 2,769.48$ cm^3	$SA = 782.28$ ft.^{2} $V = 972$ ft.^{3}	$SA = 240.21$ ft.^{2} $V = 235.5$ ft.^{3}

Notes

Notes